FOCUS ON

IELTS Foundation

TEACHER'S BOOK

PEARSON
Longman

SUE O'CONNELL

Pearson Education Limited
Edinburgh Gate
Harlow
Essex CM20 2JE
England
and Associated Companies throughout the world.

www.longman.com

First published 2007

ISBN-13: 978-0-582-82915-2
ISBN-10: 0-582-82915-1

Set in 10/12pt Times New Roman

Printed in Great Britain by Scotprint, Haddington

Designed by Linda Reed and Associates

Cover photo © Antonio M Rosario (Iconica/Getty Images)

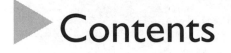

Contents

Introduction		page 4
Unit 1	Read all about it!	page 7
Key		*page 9*
Unit 2	Take note	page 11
Key		*page 13*
Unit 3	It goes with the job	page 15
Key		*page 17*
Unit 4	Family values	page 19
Key		*page 21*
Unit 5	A sporting chance	page 23
Key		*page 25*
Unit 6	Animal rights and wrongs	page 26
Key		*page 30*
Unit 7	Appropriate technology	page 32
Key		*page 34*
Unit 8	Communications	page 36
Key		*page 38*
Unit 9	Earth matters	page 40
Key		*page 42*
Unit 10	Health check	page 43
Key		*page 45*
Unit 11	Science of happiness	page 47
Key		*page 49*
Unit 12	Buildings and structures	page 51
Key		*page 54*
Writing practice bank *Key and notes*		page 55
Audio script		page 59

Introduction

Focus on IELTS Foundation is a complete course which provides a solid grounding in the key language and skills needed for success in the IELTS test. It is ideal preparation for a higher level exam course such as *Focus on IELTS*, enabling mid- or lower intermediate students to improve their performance in the final exam. When time is more limited, *Focus on IELTS Foundation* can also be used independently.

The course contains essential information and advice about the IELTS test. It is primarily designed for students aiming at the Academic modules, but much of the practice will also be relevant for those with a General Training goal.

The *Key language bank* and the *Writing practice bank* in the end section provide supplementary practice which is suitable for individual or class use. This allows teachers maximum flexibility in tailoring the course to meet their students' particular needs.

Key features of the course

- Emphasis on building accuracy and confidence in a range of **core language**

- **Exam Links** show how practice activities relate to specific exam tasks.

- **Essential language** boxes highlight core language for speaking and writing.

- **DIY Learning strategies** develop key study skills which help students progress more rapidly.

- **IELTS Vocabulary Builder** sections build up students' repertoire of core vocabulary.

- **Academic Word Study** sections focus on the most common words in academic English.

- **Review sections** consolidate key language.

- **Key language bank** provides reference and extra practice in core areas of grammar.

- **Writing practice bank** provides guided practice in additional writing topics.

Structure

The course begins with an *Overview* of the exam, which provides at-a-glance information about the overall organisation of the IELTS test, as well as details of the four modules.

This is followed by twelve teaching units divided into pairs. Odd-numbered units (1, 3, etc.) focus mainly on reading, while even-numbered units (2, 4, etc.) focus mainly on listening and writing. There is also a variety of speaking, grammar and vocabulary practice in both odd- and even-numbered units.

Every two units there is an *Academic Word Study* section, which focuses on the most common academic vocabulary, and a *Review* unit, designed to consolidate key language and exam skills. These sections are suitable for class use or homework, depending on the time available.

Each unit begins with an outline of the key skills and language practice, as well as the main exam focus. This is followed by a *Lead-in* section, which explores students' awareness of the unit theme and topic vocabulary. The *Map of the Book* on pages 2 and 3 of the Student's Book gives details of the unit-by-unit contents, and there is a full description of each component in the **Unit contents** section below.

The end section of the book contains an introduction to the *Academic Word List (AWL)* including a list of words from the AWL which are featured in the course, the *Key language bank*, and the *Writing practice bank*. There are also *Answer keys* to selected exercises in the units, and an *Audio script* for all the *Focus on listening* sections.

How to use the course

The material has been designed to be as flexible as possible, so that the time needed to work through the course can be adjusted to suit a range of teaching circumstances.

The minimum time needed to complete the course is about 60 hours. This assumes that the teacher will concentrate on core content, and that students will work through most of the *Academic Word Study* and *Review* sections on their own, using the keys at the end of the Student's Book. The *Key language bank* and *Writing practice bank* are also suitable for use as self-study resources. When time is less critical and it's possible for most of the work, including selected supplementary practice exercises, to be done in class, the material is likely to occupy 100+ hours.

The *Overview* of the exam on pages 4 and 5 is intended to give students at the start of their course a general idea of how the exam is organised and the goal they need to reach. While too much emphasis on the exam could be counterproductive, especially in the early stages of the course, the *Overview* is a useful reference point for students as they become more concerned about the exact requirements of the IELTS test in terms of task types, timings and assessment criteria.

The course is graded so that texts and tasks get more difficult as students progress. Each module of the exam is introduced in an *Exam Link*, and *Task approach* sections outline strategies for tackling individual questions.

The IELTS test is a challenging exam, particularly for lower level students, and no course, however thorough, can satisfy every learner's needs. For this reason, it's important to encourage students to take responsibility for their own learning. The *DIY Learning strategy* sections introduce key study skills to help them in this, and students should also be encouraged to make effective use of the resources in the book including the *Academic Word Study* and *Review* sections, and the *Key language bank* and *Writing practice bank,* which are designed to be used for individualised study.

Unit contents

Lead-ins

These sections serve as an introduction to the topic and an important foundation for the activities in the unit. They allow students to share any knowledge or experience they may have, to practise their communicative skills, and to extend their range of topic vocabulary. They include a variety of discussion topics, quizzes and problem solving tasks.

Focus on reading

Among the problems for lower level students preparing for the IELTS reading module are inexperience in dealing with long texts and a fear of unknown words. *Focus on IELTS* Foundation employs a step-by-step approach to build confidence and reading proficiency. There is a gradual increase in text length and complexity from shorter extracts designed to practise specific reading strategies to longer, more challenging texts with guided exam tasks.

The reading texts come from a variety of sources including newspapers, professional journals and the Internet, and a full range of reading skills are practised. Each of the main exam task types is introduced in an *Exam Link*.

Focus on speaking

Students need a wide range of speaking skills in order to do well in the IELTS test. For example, in parts 1 and 2 of the Speaking module, they may need to give information about themselves or someone they know, to express and justify an opinion, or to describe a place or event. In part

3, they have to discuss more abstract concepts, such as possible future developments or suggested solutions to a problem. They must also demonstrate an adequate range of grammar and vocabulary, together with acceptable fluency and pronunciation.

Focus on IELTS Foundation has a wide range of oral activities, including discussion, problem solving and games, designed to motivate learners and build up their confidence and fluency. Each of the three parts of the Speaking module is introduced in an *Exam Link*, and key expressions are clearly presented in *Essential language* boxes.

Focus on listening

The IELTS Listening module can often seem particularly daunting to lower level learners because it requires them to rely on their ears alone, with no visual clues to understanding, and also because the recording is heard only once. In *Focus on IELTS Foundation*, key listening sub-skills are systematically developed, and the listening tasks are carefully graded to build confidence. *Exam Links* introduce each section of the Listening module and offer practical advice.

The twenty four listening texts provide balanced coverage of the four sections of the Listening module and represent a wide variety of speech situations, both formal and informal, and a variety of accents, as in the exam itself. The audio scripts are reproduced at the end of the Student's book and on page 59 in this book.

Focus on writing

Lower level learners often have an inadequate control of basic sentence structures and need to work on this area before moving on to task-specific skills such as presenting data or structuring an argument. In *Focus on IELTS Foundation* there is an emphasis on building accuracy in a limited range of relevant language and a step-by-step approach to basic writing skills including linking and paragraphing.

There is thorough preparation for Task 1 and Task 2 of the Academic Writing module. Each task is introduced in an *Exam Link*, and key skills are built up systematically. Core language for each task is clearly presented in *Essential language* boxes.

The *Writing practice bank* provides model answers and additional writing practice suitable for class use or self-study (see below).

Focus on grammar

The *Focus on grammar* sections are designed to specifically target those core structures which are indispensable for speaking and writing tasks in the IELTS exam. This is a 'no frills' approach which deliberately omits any language which is less than essential. The aim is to avoid the confusion which can arise when a wide range of grammar is only half-learnt, and to build up a reliable repertoire of basic sentence structures which is manageable, flexible and gives lower level learners a realistic chance of achieving acceptable fluency and accuracy.

The *Focus on grammar* sections are generally designed as revision. When learners are less confident in a particular area of language, it will probably be necessary to provide extra support and a more step-by-step approach. Students can also be referred to the more detailed information and practice exercises in the *Key language bank* if necessary (see below).

DIY Learning strategy

These six sections help students to develop key study skills that will enable them to learn more effectively both in and outside class, and will also stand them in good stead in their future studies. Each section provides clear guidelines for a particular strategy and includes a *DIY Learning project*, which is an opportunity to experiment with new learning techniques in a practical way. Students are encouraged to discuss results afterwards with their peers and/or their teacher.

IELTS Vocabulary Builder

IELTS candidates need to build up a solid base of vocabulary for speaking and writing in order to express themselves on issues ranging from the personal and familiar to the more formal and abstract. To do this they need to acquire vocabulary systematically, record it efficiently (see DIY Learning page 64), and be aware how to use it. To retain new vocabulary they will also need to revisit it a number of times.

The *IELTS Vocabulary Builder* sections, which come at the end of each unit, present a range of basic topic vocabulary and also practise various key aspects of word knowledge, including meaning, register, spelling, collocation and phonology. Selected items are later revised in the *Review* sections (see below).

Academic Word Study

These sections, colour-coded yellow, occur every two units, and focus on key vocabulary from the Academic Word List (AWL), a list of the most common words in academic texts. This is an extremely valuable resource, which makes it possible to target the key vocabulary learners need to learn in order to improve their reading and writing in the IELTS test. There is more information about what the AWL is and why it's important on pages 138 and 139, and it would be helpful for students to study this before they tackle the first *Academic Word Study* section.

A list of all the AWL words included in the *Academic Word Study* sections appears on pages 138 and 139, and

there is a key to the exercises at the end of the Student's book, enabling students to use the *Academic Word Study* sections for self-study on more intensive courses.

Review

These sections, colour-coded blue, also occur every two units. They are designed to recycle key language and vocabulary and revise exam skills, in order to aid retention, provide feedback on learning and build self-confidence. Typical topics include irregular verbs, grammatical patterns, word choice and spelling. A variety of task types is used, including correction, completion, multiple choice and True/False.

There is a key to the *Review* sections at the end of the Student's book, which makes it possible for students to use this section for self-study on more intensive courses.

Practice banks

The two practice banks contain supplementary activities that can be used in a number of ways, depending on the time available. On very intensive courses, they can be treated as self-access resources. On more extended courses, you may choose to include most of these tasks in class time. On all other courses they can be used as and when the need arises, for example, for homework or for revision/remedial teaching. They are also designed to meet the needs of individual students. Each *Key language* and *Writing practice* exercise is cross-referenced in the relevant unit.

The ***Key language bank*** is set out in alphabetical order from Adverbs to Relative clauses. It contains notes on a range of key grammatical structures, together with practice exercises. It is designed to support the *Focus on grammar* sections by providing more detailed information on each language area. Depending on students' needs, they could be referred to the *Key language bank* **before, during** or **after** a *Focus on grammar* section. In other words, the Key language bank can be used as an initial introduction to an area of grammar, as a reference point for checking answers, and also as a source of further practice.

The *Just Remember* boxes are a useful feature, offering 'bottom line' advice on key points to remember and common mistakes to avoid. The answers to the exercises in the *Key language bank* can be found at the end of the Student's book.

The ***Writing practice bank*** contains ten supplementary writing exercises including gapped model answers for selected tasks, together with questions focusing on key features of organisation and language, and on the criteria for assessment. It also includes additional writing topics. A key to the exercises in the *Writing practice bank* can be found on page 55 of this book.

1 ▶ Read all about it

To set the ball rolling ...

Discuss students' reading habits. Ask them to suggest as many things as possible that they read, in addition to newspapers and books (e.g. adverts, instructions, emails, etc). Write up a few questions such as those below and ask students to discuss them in pairs. Monitor progress and note how students are coping with the range of structures involved. Finish with a brief whole-class recap.

- What was your favourite book as a child?
- What would you take to read on a long journey?
- What is the next thing you'll read after this class?

Lead-in (p. 6)

favourite

1 The aim of this task is to underline the fact that we read in different ways, depending on what we're reading and why. It's worth making this explicit and pointing out that it applies to the IELTS exam as well. Different exam questions require different reading techniques, and these will be introduced and practised during the course.

Use the first picture as an example, and ask students to suggest reasons for reading. Encourage a variety of answers if possible. Monitor students' conversations as they discuss the other pictures and invite a few pairs to talk about their ideas afterwards.

If you have time, you could usefully expand this phase to generate extra speaking and vocabulary practice. Ask students to think beyond the most obvious possibility and to create mini scenarios, e.g. A The man is going to an important interview (what for?) and he's just missed his train (why?). He's looking to see when the next one is, etc. Other possibilities include train arrival times (someone important wasn't on the train), flight departure/arrival times, stock market prices, etc. Take the opportunity to elicit relevant vocabulary e.g. A *TV monitor/screen, arrival/departure;* B *look through, the news/sports/entertainment section, catch up on the (latest) news;* C *make notes, revise/revision,* D *check email, surf the net;* E *guidebook;* F *advertisement, shop window,* etc.

2 These questions provide useful practice in some key structures. Monitor students' conversations and make a note of any remedial work you think necessary. Follow up on any interesting points afterwards.

Focus on grammar *Present simple (p. 7)*

Make a point of reading through the Exam Link and reinforcing this important message: The present and past are far more important than all the other tenses put together, so time spent learning to use these tenses accurately is definitely time well spent.

1 This task is designed as revision. If your students are less confident with basic grammar, you may need to provide extra support and a more step-by-step approach. You may also prefer lower level students to work through the section on the present simple in the Key language bank (p. 153) before continuing. That section also includes notes on question formation.

2 Students can usefully work together on this. If they need more support, ask them to identify the four correct sentences first.

3 Once students have finished let them compare sentences in pairs. Ask one of each pair to tell the class something they've learnt about their partner. Allow time for remedial work, reminding students again, if need be, how useful practice in this area of language is.

4 Focus on the Essential language first, and make sure students can use the phrases appropriately and confidently. Practise stress and intonation if necessary. Monitor the pairwork and encourage students to develop each topic a little.

Language check (spend time) + ...-ing

This structure is useful for many Interview questions and worth highlighting at this early stage. With lower level students you could make a mini teaching point of it by providing extra prompts such as: travelling to work or college/sleeping at night/exercising every week/getting ready in the morning/studying at weekends, etc.

Focus on reading 1 *Introducing reading skills (p. 8)*

This section has notes (printed in blue) on skimming, scanning and reading for detail. In each case, read through the notes as a class, making sure students understand exactly what each skill is and also how it is relevant to the IELTS test.

1 To reinforce the time-saving element of skimming, it's a good idea to set a time limit for the first task. Monitor to ensure that everyone is working at a reasonable speed, and to discourage detailed reading. Allow students to compare answers for a few moments before checking. Ask students to look back at each extract and say what clues they used to identify the topic (e.g. headings in bold + specific vocabulary items).

2 These exercises should go more quickly now that students have an overview of the extracts. Again set a fairly tight time limit for exercise 2 and monitor progress. Avoid discussing the extracts in more detail when you check answers, as this would require reading for detail, which is introduced in the next exercise.

3 It's a good idea to get students to write the number of the extract concerned for each statement. This will make it easier for them to locate information in order to discuss and justify their answers. Discuss the extracts in more detail as you check answers.

4 **Guessing unknown vocabulary**
It is very helpful if students can complete the Parts of Speech section in the Key language bank (p. 147) before they begin. This exercise introduces an important reading skill and is a valuable foundation for work on more challenging reading texts later on. When checking, ask students to identify the parts of speech and also to explain as far as possible how the context helped them guess the meaning. Check and clarify meanings further as necessary.

DIY Learning strategy
Introduction (p. 11)

This section encourages students to become more aware of their strengths and weaknesses as language learners, and to take steps to work on areas for improvement. Hopefully this introductory discussion will mark the start of an on-going dialogue about language and learning, where students feel free to voice any concerns they may have about their progress, and where they also work to help and encourage one other.

Ask students to read through the speech bubbles and let them discuss their thoughts in pairs for a few moments. Canvass opinions briefly and note any particular concerns the class has. Invite a few suggestions as to how to deal with the problems mentioned. Finally read through the notes as a class and emphasise the importance of helping yourself.

Find time for reading
Begin by finding out what kind of things (if any) students currently read in English, and ask them for more ideas about what they could usefully read. Use this phase to broaden students' view of 'reading practice' and to encourage experimentation. Read through the introduction and 'rules' and discuss each point in a little more detail. NB Ways of recording useful expressions are discussed in the DIY section on p. 64.

Introduce the DIY Learning project as a task which will help students develop the skills to help themselves as learners. Let them read through the instructions and make sure they are completely clear about what they have to do. It would be useful to allow a little time for them to decide on what to read, and it might also be helpful to have a few suitable newspapers, magazines or books on hand for those who are short of ideas or who might have difficulty accessing suitable material. To encourage commitment, make a note of each person's choice and set a specific deadline to discuss results.

Note that students need to have completed their DIY Learning project before you tackle the *Focus on speaking* section on p. 14, so the deadline should be before you plan to reach that section.

Focus on reading 2 *Reading academic texts (p. 12)*

1 Read through the instructions and emphasise the need to complete the task quickly. Give students enough time to look through the extracts fairly quickly and stop them even if some haven't completed the task. Let them compare results in pairs before checking. Finally, ask them to say which reading skills they used (skimming).

2 This task should also be answered as quickly as possible. Ask students to read through the questions and say which reading skills they need to use (scanning).
NB Extract B contains an example of referencing which may be useful to focus on as a common feature of academic writing. Mention that somewhere in extract B there's the name of an expert who has written on the subject. Ask for the name (Buzan) and what the numbers refer to (the publication date of a book or article and page number). It may also be appropriate to point out that students are normally expected to state the sources of their ideas/information in academic writing, either in this way or as part of a bibliography.

3 This is a very basic introduction to the topic, which will be developed further in later units. If students are new to the concept of reference links, it may be helpful for them to work in pairs, or to do this together as a class.

4 Make sure that students have read and understood the instructions. Ask them to say which reading skills they need to use (reading for detail). Let them compare answers before checking.

Focus on speaking *Discussing a topic (p. 14)*

Make sure that students know they need to come prepared to talk about the DIY Learning project before you reach this section!

1 Although this may look a bit like an exam task, it's not meant to be treated as exam practice. There is no need for a time limit and students can feel free to interrupt and ask questions as they wish, since this will make the experience more relaxing and natural. Ask students to report back on what their partner told them.

2 Check on chosen words and expressions with each pair and maybe have a class round-up of an interesting selection of these.

Desert island dilemma

Focus on the Essential language first, and make sure students can use the phrases appropriately and confidently. Practise stress and intonation if necessary. Rearrange seating if possible so students can easily

communicate with other members of their group. Give them time to read through the instructions and options, and check if they have any questions before beginning. While discussions are in progress, monitor to make sure that they are working towards a group choice, and note any language areas in need of attention.

IELTS Vocabulary Builder *(p. 15)*

The exercises in this section can either be completed for homework or in class time.

4 Optional additional exercise
If your students find the syllable task fairly easy you could introduce them to word stress.

1 Ask them to look at the 2-syllable words. Explain that they all have the same stress pattern: Oo (e.g. STUdy, CAREful). Practise pronouncing these words. It's worth pointing out that this is not the only stress pattern possible, many common 2-syllable words like *before* or *decide* have the pattern oO.

2 Move on to the 3- syllable words and explain that some of these have the pattern oOo (e.g. RemEMber, deCIsion), while others have the pattern Ooo (e.g. SYLLable, INterview). Ask them to decide which pattern the words in this group follow.

Encourage students to be aware of and make a note of the stress pattern of new words when they record them.

Answers
develop oOo, difficult Ooo, encourage oOo, interview Ooo, telephone Ooo

---

Unit 1 Key

Lead-in *(p.6)*
1 *Example answers*
  A Information on a TV screen (or monitor) at a railway station or airport. To check travel information e.g. train or flight departure times.
  B A newspaper. To catch up on the latest news, study the job advertisements, or just pass the time.
  C A textbook. To revise for an exam or make notes for an essay.
  D A computer screen. To check email, or use the Internet to research a project or book a holiday.
  E A guidebook. To study the history of a tourist sight, to find out the most important things to see.
  F Advertisements in a shop window. To find a cheap holiday/a job/accommodation.

Focus on grammar *(p. 7)*
1 1 e); is going on at the moment
  2 a) regularly; f)
  2 b) c)
  2 c) d) or h)
  3 Adverbs
2 1 ✓
  2 She speaks Arabic well.
  3 What does this word mean?
  4 ✓
  5 The rains often begin in July.
  6 ✓
  7 He watches too much TV
  8 ✓

Focus on reading 1 *(p. 8)*
1 1 I, N **2** G, O **3** E, J **4** H, K, L **5** B, D
  6 A, C **7** F, M

2 1 São Paolo (*Extract* F)
  2 6.5 hours (J)
  3 *Opportunity* (G)
  4 October (O)
  5 58 hours a week (B)
  6 86 years (E)
  7 tomato sauce (D)
  8 $1.9 billion (L)

3 1 True (M)
  2 False – A third of over-55s … almost the same as
    15–24 year olds (C)
  3 False – the launch was a fortnight late (G)
  4 True (H)
  5 True 'A record 437,615 people applied to begin
    degree courses …' (I)
  6 False – teachers and other workers raised the
    money (N)

4 1 too quiet to be heard
  2 likely to suffer from
  3 organise an activity so that people work well
    together effectively
  4 at a high level
  5 arresting

Focus on reading 2 *(p. 12)*

1 B reading speed
  C signalling words
  D jargon/specialist vocabulary

2 1 B 2 C 3 D 4 A

3 1 to extract deeper meaning
  2 reading slightly faster
  3 signalling words
  4 ignore jargon/difficult language and continue
    reading

4 1 skimming (skills)
  2 question
  3 every word
  4 faster
  5 lines
  6 *In summary/Finally/By contrast*
  7 organisation/structure
  8 ignore

IELTS Vocabulary Builder *(p. 15)*

1 1 admission (*Example*)
  2 announcement (also an announcer, a person
    who reads news or information on TV or radio)
  3 appearance
  4 application (also applicant, a person who applies
    for a job, university place, etc.)
  5 assistance (also assistant, a person who assists)
  6 cancellation
  7 development (also developer, a person or
    company that makes money by buying land and
    building houses, shops or factories on it)
  8 employment (also employer, a person who
    employs people, and employee, someone who is
    employed)
  9 encouragement
  10 prediction
  11 resistance
  12 solution

2 1 predictions
  2 announcement
  3 solutions
  4 admission
  5 employment; resistance

3 1 on; as 2 as 3 at 4 for 5 by 6 from
  7 from 8 for 9 to 10 in

4 **1-syllable words:** cheap, law, solve, time, train
  2-syllable words: breakfast, country, detail, future,
  taxi
  3-syllable words: develop, difficult, encourage,
  interview, telephone

2 ▶ Take note

To set the ball rolling ...

Discuss students' listening preferences briefly, either in pairs or as a class.

• Do you prefer listening to the news on the radio or watching it on TV? (why?)

• What kind of music do you play while you study? Or do you prefer silence?

• What everyday sounds really annoy you? (e.g. car alarms, someone listening to an MP3 player at maximum volume)

• What everyday sounds do you like most?

• What makes a 'good listener'?

• What kind of things does a 'bad listener' do?

Lead-in (p. 16)

Ask students to work through exercises 1 and 2 and check answers. Point out that, as with reading, we listen in different ways depending on what we're listening to and why, and that this also applies to the IELTS exam. Different exam questions require different listening techniques, and these will be introduced and practised during the course. Give students time to discuss question 3 and invite brief feedback.

Focus on listening 1 Letters and sounds 1 (p. 17)

Key phonemic symbols are introduced gradually during the course as a way of helping students identify and refer to specific sounds. Familiarity with phonemic symbols will also help them understand the pronunciation information in dictionaries. Unless students are already familiar with these symbols, it's worth spending time practising each sound here thoroughly, and revising from time to time later.

Focus on speaking Discussing likes and dislikes (p. 17)

Focus on the Essential language first, and make sure students can use the phrases appropriately and confidently. Practise stress and intonation if necessary, using a different topic such as leisure activities or musical tastes.

1 Ask students to work in pairs and provide a suitable prompt question e.g. 'Do you often read ...?' Or 'Do you like reading ...? to start the conversations. Monitor the pairwork and encourage students to extend their answers a little, if possible, by giving reasons or examples.

2 This is intended as a gentle introduction to the first part of the Speaking test (see p. 6). While it's not meant to be serious exam practice, it's worth introducing a little formality into the activity by asking pairs to sit facing each other if possible.

Read through the Exam Link and point out that the main aim of the task is to practise this key language. Check that students have chosen a set of questions and are clear about what they have to do. Monitor the interviews, helping as necessary, and note areas for remedial work.

Focus on listening 2 Introducing listening skills (p. 18)

Start by recapping the reading skills of skimming and scanning so that students can see the parallels with the listening skills introduced here.

Make sure that everyone is clear about exactly what's required in each task before playing the recording. Depending on your students' ability, you may want to help them along a little by establishing the correct answer for the first extract (public announcement) as an introduction. NB In exercise 3 it's worth clarifying that only a number is required, not the unit (dollars, degrees etc.).

Give students time to compare answers before checking, and follow up with some post-listening questions exploring which questions students found easiest and which hardest, and why.

Focus on grammar Expressing frequency (p. 19)

Read through the Exam Link first. With stronger students you could consider beginning with exercise 2, using it as a diagnostic test to indicate how much work is needed in this language area. With lower level students, you will need to work through section 1 carefully, as suggested below. Note that there is detailed information on adverbs in the Key language bank on p. 140.

1 Give students time to read through the introduction and tables, then ask them to suggest possible expressions to complete the three example sentences, e.g. **Initial** *Sometimes/Occasionally/Once in a while* Make sure they are completely clear about how the table is organised before continuing.

Questions 1 and 2 provide a very useful tip, especially for lower level students for whom the range of options can seem bewildering. Give them time to consider the question but help them to the right conclusion if necessary. The middle position is safest because it is correct not only for 'middle position only' adverbs but also for 'all three positions' adverbs. Only adverbs of exact frequency and longer time expressions cannot appear in that position.

NB Negative expressions like *never* and *hardly ever* are sometimes used at the beginning of sentences in a special structure where the verb and subject are inverted. However, this is not part of the basic repertoire required at this level and is also potentially confusing, so it is not included here.

2 Allow time for students to check the sentences with reference to the information in the table and let them compare results in pairs. When checking, make sure they justify their answers by referring to the table.

3/4 For maximum talking time, both these exercises could be done in pairs with a brief open class stage. Exercise 4 could also be treated as a gentle introduction to Part 2 of the Speaking test (which is formally introduced in the Exam Link on p. 30).

5 Let students read through the instructions and check that they understand how the game will work. Organise small groups and allow time for students to compose three statements about themselves. It's best to check these quickly for accuracy if possible before beginning the activity. Monitor and note language areas for remedial practice.

Focus on writing 1 *Introduction to Task 1 (p. 20)*

1/2 Read through the Exam Link and give students time to study extracts A–F. Let them compare ideas for Exercises 1 and 2 in pairs before checking answers as a class. It would be useful to focus on some basic aspects of register and writing style in relation to academic English before moving on.

3 Read through the Exam Link as a class and then ask students to tackle Exercise 3 individually before comparing answers and working out corrections in pairs.

4 Let students study the Essential language and give extra practice if necessary using prompts such as:

- Population: UK (60 million) v Egypt (65.7 million);
- Airport Passengers: Changi, Singapore (24m) v Kimpo, S Korea (29m)
- Percentage of young children in primary education: Greece (91) v Malaysia (91)
- Daily newspapers: Germany (375) v India (3037)
- Tourists visiting each year: Mexico (19.4 m) v France (66.9 m)

Allow time for students to prepare suitable statements and check these for grammatical accuracy if possible before continuing.

5/6 Let students compare answers before checking Exercise 5 and encourage them to use this as a model for describing diagram D.

DIY Learning strategy *Good learning habits (p. 22)*

This section encourages students to consider different approaches to learning and to broaden their own range of learning strategies.

1 Remind students about the frequency expressions from the Focus on grammar section on p. 19 and recap briefly, if necessary. Point out that this activity is an opportunity to practise this language as well as discussing good learning habits. Make sure students can form questions (*How often do you …/Do you … much?*) confidently and correctly before beginning.

2/3 Once students have discussed these points in pairs, open up a class discussion. It's important not to be too prescriptive but to accept that everyone has different learning styles and that what works for one person may not work for another. The key thing is to focus on the advantages of the good learning habits and to encourage students to experiment with one or two that they don't do on a regular basis.

For the DIY Learning project, make sure students have chosen a specific activity and have some practical ideas for implementing it. Put a date in your diary to discuss results in pairs and as a class (and also to encourage students to keep up the good work!)

Focus on writing 2 *Task 2 (p. 23)*

Read through the Exam Link and then let students work through each section, either individually or in pairs. Check answers as you go, discussing and clarifying the points as necessary.

NB When students have completed Exercise 6, it would be useful for them to look at the model answer in the Writing practice bank (p. 156), so they have a clear idea of what they need to aim at in a Task 2 answer.

The model answer is followed by questions focussing on organisation and language features, which relate directly to the Focus on writing sections, so it would be good if students could complete these as soon as possible, perhaps for homework. There are teaching notes and a key to the questions in this book (p. 55).

IELTS Vocabulary Builder (p. 25)

The exercises in this section can either be completed for homework or in class time.

Unit 2 Key

Lead-in (p. 16)
1 1 D 2 E 3 B 4 A (*Example*) 5 C 6 F
2 *Suggested answers*
  1 1, 3
  2 1 (when face to face), (3), 4
  3 1 (when face to face) gestures for 'turn left', 'like this', etc; 2 (if on TV) picture, diagrams, etc; 3 notes on board, slides, etc; 4 (when face to face) facial expression, gesture, etc;
  4 2 (when interested in specific items), 5, 6 (e.g. when concerning several journeys)
  5 2, 5 (when driving), 6

Focus on listening 1 (p. 17)
1

/iː/	/eɪ/
1 three	**2** eight
3 B C D E G P T V	**4** A H J K

2 1 C 2 B 3 A 4 B
3 1 TOAD HALL
  2 SANDRINGHAM
  3 MANSFIELD PARK

Focus on listening 2 (p. 18)
1 1 i 2 d 3 h 4 b 5 g
2 1 Paris
  2 Sydney
  3 Japan
  4 Washington
  5 India
3 1 15 (degrees)
  2 ($) 800
  3 12 (per cent/%)
  4 57 million
  5 1903

Focus on grammar (p. 19)
1 1 Middle position
  2 Adverbs of exact frequency (e.g. *once a week*) and longer expressions generally.

2 1 I <u>can never remember</u> your address.
  2 ✓
  3 ✓
  4 He <u>hardly ever sleeps</u> more than five hours.
  5 She <u>is never</u> in her office when I phone.
  6 You <u>must always</u> read the instructions.
  7 ✓
  8 The company <u>holds a staff party every year/ Every year the company holds</u> a staff party …

Focus on writing 1 (p. 20)
1 **A** Part of a personal letter or note. Notice typical features such as informal expressions (*thrilled to bits, I'm dying to hear*); informal structures (*And what about …*) and incomplete sentences (*Can't remember*). This is <u>not</u> an IELTS writing task type.
  B Part of a discussion essay. This could be from a Task 2 answer in the Academic version of the IELTS writing paper.
  C Study notes from a lecture or a text book. This is not an IELTS writing task type, although notes like these might appear in a completion task in the listening module.
  D Part of <u>a description</u> of how something works. The use of the letters A and B tells us that this would accompany a diagram. This could also be from a Task 1 answer in the Academic version of IELTS writing paper.
  E Part of a description of information in a graph. This could be from a Task 1 answer in the Academic version of the IELTS writing paper.
  F Part of a formal letter, probably from a student to his or her tutor, apologising and giving reasons for missing a week of term. Notice the use of fairly formal language and the absence of contractions (*I am, I will,* etc). This is a possible task in the General Training version of the IELTS test but not in the Academic version.
2 1 D, E 2 A, C 3 B, F 4 E 5 B

3 1 F Americans spend (**considerably**) **more time** …
than …
2 T
3 F People in Australia spend (**slightly**) **less time** …
than …
4 T
5 F *USA* Today has a **slightly larger** circulation …
than …

5 1 approximately/just over a third; 36 %
2 exactly a quarter/25%
3 slightly smaller/2% less
4 10%
5 6%

6 *Example answer*
The best selling quality Sunday newspaper in Britain is the *Sunday Times*, which has a market share of just under 50%. The next most popular Sunday paper is the *Sunday Telegraph* which has a market share of just over a quarter. After these two market leaders, the *Observer* and the *Independent on Sunday* have smaller market shares of 15% and 9% respectively.

Focus on writing 2 *(p. 23)*

1 1 b) **2** a) **3** d) **4** c)
2 Para 1: *At university … included.* (line 5) Topic: Types of written work required at university.
Para 2: *All pieces … tutor.* (line 8) Topic: The need to structure written work.
Para 3: *You will normally … extra ones.* (line 12) Topic: The need to stick to a word limit.
3 1 and, also
2 so, because
3 generally, normally
4 but, conversely
4 1 your tutor
2 the (writing) task
3 the appropriate structure to use
4 the number of words you should write
5 words
5 Greenland is situated in the north Atlantic. ~~Greenland~~ It has an Arctic climate and much of ~~Greenland's~~ its land is permanently covered with ice. Greenlanders are an independent people, and ~~Greenlanders~~ their origins are a mix of Inuit and European. Young ~~Greenlanders~~ people are increasingly rejecting the traditional lifestyle by moving to the towns, ~~The fact that they are rejecting the traditional lifestyle and moving to the towns~~ which/and this is becoming a problem for ~~Greenland's~~ the country's welfare system.
6 1 g) **2** d) **3** f) **4** c) **5** e) **6** a) **7** h) **8** b)

IELTS Vocabulary Builder *(p. 25)*

1 1 Sitcom (situation + comedy)
2 Soap opera
3 Reality TV
4 Chat show
5 Quiz show
6 Documentary
2 1 make **2** give **3** do **4** make **5** do **6** do
7 make **8** give **9** give **10** do **11** give
12 give **13** make **14** make
3 1 do … test/examination
2 give … advice
3 make … plan
4 make … mistakes
5 do … practice/exercises
6 give … instructions

3 ▶ It goes with the job

To set the ball rolling ...

Point out that *work* is a very common and predictable topic in the IELTS test. Find out for future reference if anyone has a job, part-time or full-time, (or who has had a job in the past).

Spend a few moments outlining some typical topic areas relating both to personal experience, relevant to Parts 1 and 2 of the Interview, and also to more abstract issues which might feature in Part 3 of the Interview or Task 2 of the Writing paper. Write these on the board (perhaps in the form of a mindplan as on p. 29) and add any useful topic vocabulary that emerges.

WORK
PERSONAL EXPERIENCE
(Speaking Parts 1 and 2)
e.g. A job you have/you have done in the past/ you hope to do in future
* *Describe a typical day*
* *What are the good/bad aspects of the job?*
etc.

GENERAL DISCUSSION POINTS
(Speaking Part 3; Writing Task 2)
* ***Sexual equality:*** *e.g. Should men and women receive equal pay for equal work?*
* ***Ageism:*** *e.g. Should people be forced to retire at a certain age?*
* ***Industrial relations:*** *Do you think essential workers like doctors and fire fighters should have the right to belong to a trade union?*
* ***Work-related health problems:*** *e.g. Is there anything employers can do to help their workers stay healthy/avoid stress?*

Lead-in *(p. 28)*

1 Check the vocabulary/pronunciation of items on the careers list as necessary (e.g. *athlete, vet = veterinary surgeon*). Give students time to discuss questions 1–3 in pairs and then open a class discussion, feeding in useful language as appropriate, e.g. *It depends on ....* (e.g. *It depends on the type of doctor*) NB This language is included in the Essential language box on p. 34.

When you have revealed the results of the survey (see Key), ask if students think the top three career choices of teenagers in their own country would be different and if so, how? You may want to discuss the fact that the results still show fairly stereotypical career choices,

despite advances in sexual equality over the last 50 years. However, you could also mention that in the very first Gallup survey in 1977, the girl's top choice was secretary, so some progress has been made!

2 Focus on the Essential language first, and point out how important this is for many discussion topics. Practise the language using different prompts such as: Which of the careers would:
* need the longest training?
* be the most physically demanding?
* be most difficult for the person's family?

Make sure students can use the phrases appropriately and confidently before continuing. Monitor the pairwork and encourage students to give detailed reasons for their answers.

Focus on speaking 1 *Discussing jobs and careers (p. 29)*

1 Ask students to study the Essential language and give brief practice using unusual occupations such as clown, spy, burglar, queen, etc.

2 Let students study the mindplan and check vocabulary as necessary. On the board draw up a similar mindplan for your job as a teacher (or some other more exciting job from your past!) Write the job title and get students to ask two or three questions based on prompts from the book, to show the kind of questions that can be asked and the kind of information that can be given. Point out how they can extend a line of questioning, e.g. Where did you study? How long was the course? Underline the need to use an appropriate tense, whether past simple to describe a job now finished, or present/present perfect to describe an ongoing job.

3/4 Monitor pair work and note any language areas which need remedial work.

Focus on reading 1 *My worst job (p. 30)*

Students often miss quite obvious information in reading texts because they begin reading in detail immediately. Start by asking a few basic questions to focus students' attention on the general picture and the way the information is organised, e.g. What is the topic? How many people are featured? How old is Nadine Theron? What else can you tell me about her? (job, city, country)

1 Emphasise the need for efficient reading. Advise students to read only the first few lines of each text, looking for the name of a job or place of work. If they can't find an answer, they should move on to the next text, thus narrowing the choices. Allow only a short time for students to choose an answer.

2 Read through the advice in the Exam Link first. Advise students to underline key words in the questions before starting and do this as a class for the first few by way of encouragement. Emphasise that they need to read quickly, looking for the facts they need and ignoring all other information. You could also suggest they look for any questions with names in them and write the letter of the appropriate text next to these. That way, they can do all the questions relating to a particular text together.

3 Again, ask students to underline key words, on their own this time. Remind them of the advice in the Exam Link on p. 31 and suggest they look through all the questions before starting and begin by answering the easy ones. Once they've done that, they can re-read more carefully to answer the remaining questions.

Let students compare answers before checking and make sure they can justify their answers by reference to the text. Ask which reading skills were needed for each task.

Focus on grammar *Past simple (p. 32)*

Remind students that the past simple is one of the two key tenses in English (see Exam Link p. 7) and read through the Exam Link together first.

Use Exercise 1 for diagnostic purposes. If you find your students are fairly weak in this area of grammar, you may want them to work through the section on the past simple in the Key language bank (p. 150) before continuing.

Focus on speaking 2 *Job satisfaction (p. 34)*

Let students study the introduction and lists of workers. Check vocabulary as necessary (e.g. *nursery, civil servant, assembly line*) and perhaps draw their attention to the fact that police officers are restricted to 'sergeant and below' (i.e. jobs with limited responsibility compared to higher ranks such as inspectors).

1 1 Allow time for discussion and invite brief feedback. Then draw up a list of matching positive and negative descriptions like those below. Leave this list on the board during the next activity.

interesting/useful	boring, dead-end
varied	repetitive
well paid	poorly paid
challenging	stressful

2 Before students start, focus on the Essential language and clarify/practise as necessary, using occupations from the original list. Monitor the pairwork and encourage students to justify their opinions using relevant topic vocabulary and also to illustrate their ideas using personal examples, e.g. *I have a friend who's a ....* Use the list you made on the board (see above) to guide feedback to the discussion.

2 Read through the Exam Link and then give students about five minutes to discuss the three questions. Monitor the pairwork and have a whole-class round-up to finish.

Focus on reading 2 *Service workers are the happiest staff (p. 35)*

Ask students to look at the title of the text and point out that this article provides the background information for the table they discussed in the previous section. Clarify the term 'service workers' (waiters, cleaners, receptionists and others providing a basic service).

1–4 Before students tackle exercises 1–3, explain that they need to read the instructions and also the Tip boxes in the margin in order to find out:
- what kind of answer they need to give
- which section of the text they need to read for each group of questions
- whether the answers are in the same order as the information in the text or not (NB the information given here applies to the exam as well.)

Be sure to make it clear that this is additional help which is not available in the exam!

Point out that they must search the text for answers (rather than guess) and tell them that you will ask them to justify their answers by mentioning relevant sections of the text. Monitor carefully in order to give helpful feedback and also to steer lower level students in the right direction.

When checking, insist that students give evidence from the text to justify their answers, using line numbers, and underline the importance of noticing parallel expressions (e.g. *workers/employees*). This will be a recurring theme throughout the book.

5 Remind students what is meant by the term 'reference link' if necessary (this was introduced on p. 13).

6 It's worth spending a few moments talking about dealing with unknown vocabulary in a text. You could introduce the term *neologophobia* (fear of new words) and ask if there are any sufferers in the class! Point out that any reading passage in the exam, and any academic text, in fact, is very likely to contain a number of unknown words. Fortunately, it isn't necessary to understand every word in order to answer most exam questions.

The important thing is to recognise when a word is important to overall understanding and, if so, to know how to work out the general meaning. Check whether students remember the advice on working out meaning from p. 10, namely to use the clues provided by the part of speech and the context. This exercise provides guided practice in this technique. First ask students to find the 'problem' word or phrase in the text and to say what part of speech it is.

IELTS Vocabulary Builder *(p. 37)*

The exercises in this section can either be completed for homework or in class time.

Unit 3 Key

Lead-in *(p. 28)*

1 According to the survey, the results were as follows:
   1 Doctor/Nurse/Medical worker, Teacher, Computer specialist
   2 Computer specialist, Engineer, Soldier/army officer (these careers did not appear in the girls' top ten at all)
   3 Vet (this career did not appear in the boys' top ten at all)

Focus on reading 1 *(p. 30)*

1 1 B 2 C 3 D 4 A
2 1 Finland
   2 Physiotherapist
   3 Chen Liang
   4 By horse-drawn cart
   5 Cleaner or 'sanitary worker'
   6 German
   7 8.30 am
   8 Ten hours
3 1 B, C 2 A, D 3 B 4 A 5 D 6 A, C
   7 B 8 C 9 A 10 B

Focus on grammar *(p.32)*

1 Not in the past simple:
   4 I've lived … (present perfect simple)
   6 It was raining … (past progressive)
   7 … share prices had fallen … (past perfect)
2 1 -*d* or -*ed*; arrive<u>d</u>, miss<u>ed</u>,
   2 learn/memorise them
   3 did not (didn't)
   4 did + subject
3 1 rose
   2 began
   3 caught
   4 took; found; cost
   5 could; went
   6 spread; became
   7 fell; froze
   8 brought; made
4 1 ✓
   2 Where did you <u>stay</u>?
   3 ✓
   4 ✓
   5 I didn't <u>understand</u> the question …
   6 ✓
   7 How much <u>did you pay</u> …?
   8 The manager <u>rang</u> …

Focus on speaking 2 *(p.34)*

1 **1** *Example answers*: The 'Fun Jobs' generally involve regular contact with people. Some are particularly useful or worthwhile jobs (childcare, police officers). Most have limited responsibility (sergeant and below). The second group includes jobs with limited human contact (e.g. authors, telephone operators), jobs involving boring or repetitive work (assembly line workers) and jobs with more responsibility than the first group (bank managers).

2 Possible factors that might contribute to job satisfaction include: good working conditions, interesting/challenging/worthwhile work, variety, good relationship with boss/colleagues, etc.

The results according to the same study are as follows:

H: gardeners; **M**: airline pilots, waiters; **L**: school teachers

NB The study is described in more detail in Reading Passage 2.

Focus on reading 2 *(p. 35)*

1 **1** Britain *(line 2)*   **2** 35,000 *(5)*
   3 Michael Rose *(14–15)*
2 **1** F *(22–4)*   **2** E *(25–7)*   **3** C *(32–3)*
   4 G *(35–37)*
3 **1** T *(lines 5–7)*   **2** F *(10–13)*   **3** T *(15–16)*
   4 NG   **5** F *(34–37)*   **6** T *(40–43)*
   7 F *(46–52)*
5 **1** *employees (line 5)*
   2 *highly paid professional and managerial staff (8/9)*
   3 *a cleaner's job (17)*
   4 *Michael Rose (14)*
   5 *medical secretaries (26)*
   6 *The report (41)*
6 **1** A   **2** B   **3** A   **4** A   **5** B

IELTS Vocabulary Builder *(p. 37)*

1 **1** e)   **2** g)   **3** f)   **4** h)   **5** a)   **6** c)   **7** d)   **8** b)
2 **1** white-collar workers
   2 work experience
   3 self-employed; sick pay
   4 assembly line; working conditions
3 **1** make   **2** take   **3** do   **4** hand in; give
   5 go; met
4 **Oo**: answer, office, person, stressful, sentence, workforce
   oO: afford, although, career, employ, involve, receive

4 ▶ Family values

To set the ball rolling ...

Spend a few moments outlining some typical topic areas relating to the general theme of families/relationships/friends and write these on the board dividing them into personal and more abstract issues, perhaps in the form of a mindplan. Add any useful topic vocabulary that emerges.

FAMILIES/FRIENDS
PERSONAL EXPERIENCE
(Speaking Parts 1 and 2)

- *things you did as a child*
- *social activities you enjoy with friends*
- *a member of your family who has had an important influence on you*
- *your best friend and how you met them*

GENERAL DISCUSSION POINTS
(Speaking Part 3; Writing Task 2)

- *Marriage: e.g. the ideal age to get married*
- *Gender roles: e.g. housework/managing money*
- *Friendship: e.g. important qualities in a friend*
- *Children: e.g. Is it wrong to smack a child?*
- *The elderly: e.g. the care of old people: the family or the state?*

Alternatively you could discuss these or other appropriate quotations:

- *Your friend is the person who knows all about you and still likes you.* (Elbert Hubbard)

- *Happiness is having a large, loving, caring, close-knit family in another city.* (George Burns, American comedian)

Lead-in *(p. 38)*

1 1 Establish the terms 'extended family' and 'nuclear family'. Monitor discussions and encourage students to give examples from their own experience.

  2 Begin by reminding students of the Essential language for expressing a personal opinion (p. 14) and for speculating (p. 28). It may also be worth revising the use of *It depends* (p. 34). After the discussion ask a few pairs to report back to the class.

2 Let students share their vocabulary knowledge by comparing answers in twos or threes. Check thoroughly and then ask them to choose one or two expressions which they hadn't met before or don't normally use, and write true sentences to illustrate the meaning.

3 Check that students remember how to identify syllables in a word (this was introduced on p. 15). If they find this difficult, you could work together to supply one example in each category before they begin. Use the checking phase to practise pronunciation as necessary.

4 Allow enough time for students to give this task proper attention. Encourage them by taking an interest in the expressions they choose and allowing time for them to record them clearly. Try to make a point of finding out if they can remember the expressions, or have used them, in a few days' time.

Focus on speaking 1 *Discussing relationships (p. 39)*

Read through the Exam Link and point out how much you can help yourself by preparing for highly predictable topics like this in the interview.

1 Let students study the Essential language and highlight expressions that are relevant to their own situation. Invite them to make true statements about themselves and use this phase to practise pronunciation and build fluency and confidence. You could extend this practice by asking them to talk about a parent or best friend in the same way.

2 Make sure students understand the diagrams. If necessary, do extra examples before they start by drawing one or two more families of stick people on the board, highlighting the father and the eldest child, for example. Let students practise in pairs before checking.

3 Allow a couple of minutes for students to gather their thoughts and make a few notes, if they wish. Monitor discussions and invite one or two students to report back on what their partner has told them.

4 Remind students of the procedure in the interview (see Exam Link p. 30) and explain how important it is to cover each point on the topic card. Tell them you're going to ask them to report back on their partner's performance, and write up the following questions:

Did he/she   talk for long enough?
                mention all the points on the topic card?
                speak without too much hesitation?

Allow a minute for preparation and then monitor students' performances. Afterwards invite students to comment on their partner's performance, discouraging too much criticism and ending on a positive note.

Focus on writing 1 *Task 1: Key Skills (p. 40)*

Read through the Exam Link and make sure students are clear about the three key elements in answering a Task 1 question. Clarify *significant trend* if necessary e.g. by drawing a simple graph showing an overall upward or downward trend.

Exercises 1–3 practise each of the three elements mentioned in the Exam Link and it's worth making this explicit as you introduce each one, to make it easier for students to remember what's required in a good answer.

4 The past perfect tense has limited value where IELTS is concerned, especially if time is short, as there are very few occasions when it is absolutely necessary. However, one of these that is worth focusing on is the use of the past perfect with *by* in Task 1 answers, and the gapped text here includes three examples. You could simply focus on the form and use of the past perfect in context but, if you have more time, you may want students to look at the section on the past perfect in the Key language bank (p. 149).

NB There is further practice in interpreting data from tables in the Writing practice bank (p. 157), which students could do in class if you feel they would benefit from more practice in this area. The section also includes a gapped model answer, which is suitable for homework.

Focus on listening 1 *Letters and sounds 2 (p. 42)*

This section introduces two more key phonemic symbols. Begin by revising /iː/ and /eɪ/ from p. 17, and remind students that recognising phonemic symbols can help them record new vocabulary accurately and also use a dictionary more effectively.

Both exercises illustrate the fact that English spelling is not a very reliable guide to pronunciation and it's helpful to make this explicit. When students have completed exercise 1, draw their attention to the variety of spellings that represent each sound. Similarly, when you have checked exercise 2, ask them to count the number of spellings which can represent the sound /e/ (6).

Focus on listening 2 *International Friendship Club (p. 42)*

As this is the first exam-style listening task, it's important to concentrate on teaching rather than simply testing. You can afford to take things step-by-step, allowing plenty of time for preparation and analysis, and you could also replay sections if necessary, especially with lower level students. It's more important to build confidence at this stage than to replicate exam conditions.

1/2/3 Read through the Exam Link and introduction and discuss questions a)–d) as a class. Play the first part of the recording and check answers before continuing.

4/5/6 Let students answer questions a)–c) individually or in pairs and then read through the Exam Link. After playing the second part of the recording and checking answers, have a general class discussion about how students feel they got on and which questions they found most difficult to answer.

Focus on grammar *Articles (p. 44)*

The tasks in this section are designed as revision. If your students are less confident with basic grammar, you may need to provide extra support and a more step-by-step approach. You may also prefer lower level students to work through the section on the articles in the Key language bank (p. 141) before continuing.

1 The subject of the text has potential as a speaking topic so it's worth introducing it briefly: e.g. Is it common to eat together as a family in your country? What difference does it make if families don't eat together regularly? What is fast food? What fast food do you eat? What's wrong with fast food? etc.

Working as a class, find the first example from each of the three categories a), c) and e) and then let students find the remaining examples.

2/3 Let students compare ideas in pairs and, when checking, ask them to justify their answers by referring to the rules a)–g) or the Key language notes.

Focus on writing 2 *Task 2: Paragraphs (p. 45)*

Begin with books closed. First see if students can remember the key advice on writing a Task 2 essay from Unit 2 (p. 23, 1 questions 1–4). Write the first half of the sentences on the board and ask students to complete them, or check orally.

Next, go back to basics and find out what students understand about paragraphs. What exactly is a paragraph? Why do writers use paragraphs? How do you show that you're beginning a new paragraph? They can then open their books and check their answers by reading through the information in the Exam Link and introduction. To make sure that students are completely clear about the concepts of topic and supporting sentences, you may need to work as a class to identify these in paragraph A. After checking the others, you could usefully focus on linking, to carry on this theme from Unit 2. Ask students to underline all the linking expressions they can find and to put them under the headings: **Addition** (Answers: *and, also, not just … but also ..)*; **Generalisation** (*usually, generally*); **Contrast/ opposite idea** (*but, However*)

For exercise 3, it would be helpful to talk through each topic first and elicit a few examples of supporting ideas, as a support for lower level students. Stronger students may well come up additional ideas of their own.

Focus on speaking 2 *Dealing with difficult questions (p. 46)*

1 Focus on the Essential language first, and practise by asking some additional hard-to-answer questions (e.g. What's the best place for a tourist to visit in your country?) Focus especially on appropriate stress and intonation.

2 Monitor the pairwork and encourage students to develop each topic a little.

3 Remind students to try and use more than one way of expressing a personal opinion (see Essential language p. 14). Monitor discussions and use the feedback stage as an opportunity to input any additional relevant language

DIY Learning strategy *Listen up!* (p. 46)

This section encourages students to look for opportunities for listening practice outside class. Point out the need to listen **actively**. Firstly, they should listen for a specific purpose, whether it's to get a general idea about the weather, to check a train time, or to find out the punch line of a joke. Secondly, they need to look for clues to help them understand. In face-to-face situations, they should pay attention to facial expression and gesture, which are often used to emphasise key details. With recordings they should listen for sentence stress, also used to underline key points, and intonation.

Begin by reading through the speech bubbles. Ask students if they share any of the concerns and discuss these briefly. Then find out some of the things students listen to in English. Let them read through the 'rules' and double-check before continuing.

Once students have read the instructions for the DIY Learning project, give them time to decide on a specific type of listening in discussion with classmates and with your guidance. It would be useful to have a few spoken word tapes, CDs or DVDs on hand for those who are short of ideas or who might have difficulty accessing suitable material. To encourage commitment, make a note of each person's choice and set a specific deadline to discuss results.

IELTS Vocabulary Builder (p. 47)

The exercises in this section can either be completed for homework or in class time.

Unit 4 Key

Lead-in (p. 38)
2 1 d) 2 e) 3 g) 4 f) 5 a) 6 h) 7 b) 8 c)
3 1 best, ring, leave, friend, tree
2 wedding, married, single, status, parent, couple
3 extended, family, marital
4 maternity

Focus on speaking 1 (p. 39)
2 *Suggested answers*
a) I'm an only child.
b) I'm the youngest of three children. I've got two older sisters.
c) I'm the middle child of five. I've got an older brother and sister and two younger brothers.
d) I/we've got two children, a girl and a boy.

Focus on writing 1 (p. 40)
1 1 200/two hundred
2 7
3 number of households
4 the last column on the right
2 a)

	Most common household size	Least common household size
1790	7	1
1890	7	1
1990	2	7

b) *Example answer*
The average household size in 1990 was less than/just under half than/ the average household size in 1790.
The average household size fell by over 50 per cent over the period 1790 to 1990.

3 1 Approximately/just under/almost   half
    2 Approximately/just over   a quarter
    3 Approximately/just under/almost   a third
    4 Approximately/just over   three quarters

4 *Suggested answers*
    1 200/two hundred
    2 5.4
    3 2.6
    4 approximately/just over   a third
    5 approximately/just under   a quarter
    6 least
    7 4%/four per cent
    8 over/more than   half/50%

Focus on listening 1 *(p. 42)*

1 /aɪ/ child height flight eye quite buyer
   /eɪ/ great weight break neighbour

2 1 said   2 many   3 measure   4 friend   5 guess
    6 leisure   7 breath   8 plenty

3 1 ALBANY   2 CARLISLE
    3 MAINSTAY   4 CHANNING

Focus on listening 2 *(p. 42)*

1 *Example answers*
    a) The name of a day
    b) e.g. a magazine or leaflet
    c) adjective
    d) The answer to question 5 (3 terms in a year)

2 1 Thursday   2 newsletter   3 active   4 5   5 12

4 a) 9
    b) 6 (surname), 7 (nationality) and 8 (Street name)
    c) an academic subject

5 6 LANZERAC   7 South African   8 March
    9 22   10 Art History

Focus on grammar *(p.44)*

1 a) a recent study
    b) a meal
    c) the study
    d) the proportion of teenagers who eat fast food
      regularly
    e) families, meals
    f) life, people, time, fast food
    g) North America

2 1 ~~the~~ women … ~~the~~ men
    2 <u>a</u> serious problem
    3 to ~~the~~ Taiwan
    4 about <u>the</u> number of students
    5 ~~The~~ Life

3 1 –   2 the   3 the   4 –   5 –   6 a   7 –   8 an
    9 the   10 –   11 a   12 –

Focus on writing 2 *(p.45)*

1 *Suggested answers*
   A **Topic sentence:** '*A lecture is a talk on a particular topic given to a group of people.*' **Additional information:** the size of the audience, the main roles of lecturer and audience
   B **Topic sentence:** '*…the most important learning can take place after the work is returned to them.*' **Additional information:** what kind of things you can learn from your teacher's comments.
   C **Topic sentence:** '*Learning a language is not just a question of learning language but also of discovering how another society communicates.*' **Additional information:** problems that can occur when we don't fully understand another cultural system.

2 1 A group of people
    2 the lecture
    3 the role
    4 their essay
    5 discovering

Focus on speaking 2 *(p. 46)*

2 *Example answers*
    1 It's hard to say. It **depends on** the time of year/the kind of holiday you enjoy; It **depends when** you plan to visit; It **depends what** you want to do, etc.
    2 It's hard to say. It **depends on** the type of hotel you like; It **depends if** you prefer a luxury hotel or a budget hotel. It **depends how much** you want to spend, etc.
    3 It's hard to say. It **depends on** the individual student; It **depends how** intensive the course is; It **depends how much** you study every day. It **depends if** you are living in the country or not, etc.

IELTS Vocabulary Builder *(p. 47)*

1 1 uncle   2 cousin   3 sister-in-law
    4 brother-in-law   5 daughter   6 nephew

2 1 bride's   2 honeymoon   3 separate   4 ex-wife
    5 partner

3 1 bravery   2 engagement   3 generosity
    4 height   5 honesty   6 kindness   7 loyalty
    8 reliability   9 responsibility   10 warmth

5 ▶ A sporting chance

To set the ball rolling ...

If there is space in your classroom for students to mingle, you could begin with a 'Find someone who ...' activity. Prepare a list of points which will prompt questions with a good mix of structures (see examples below). It's best to have slightly fewer points than the number of students in the class, unless you have a very small class! For example:

Find someone who...
> takes part in a sport regularly
> played in their school sports team
> has had a sports injury
> prefers watching sport to taking part in it
> hates sport
> has won a medal or prize for sport
> is a very keen football fan
> enjoys a water sport

Explain the procedure. The aim is to find someone who matches each of the points in the list. To do this, students have to move around and ask questions. When they get a positive answer, they should write that student's name next to the prompt.

The main rules are that they must ask correct questions and that they can only ask each student one question before moving on. The completed list should have as many different names as possible. It's best to monitor from the sidelines (unless you are needed to make up numbers!) Afterwards you could follow up any interesting points in a general class discussion.

Lead-in (p. 50)

1 Ask students to name the sports shown in the pictures (they can use the list of athletes given for guidance if necessary). Check understanding of the remaining sports.

Ensure that students understand the instructions and ask them to work in pairs to complete the table. When checking answers, ask pairs to give brief reasons for their decisions.

Notes
* *strenuous* means 'needing a lot of effort or strength'.
* a *decathlete* is a man competing in the decathlon, which covers ten events: 100 metres, long jump, shot put, high jump, 400 metres (day one), 110 metres hurdles, discus, pole vault, javelin, 1,500 metres (day two). Women compete in the heptathlon, which covers seven events (not including discus and pole vault).

* The *Tour de France* is a French road race for professional cyclists, held every year. It covers approximately 4,800 km and takes three weeks to complete.

2 Monitor the pair discussions and follow up with a feedback phase taking the opportunity to input any additional relevant language.

Focus on Speaking 1 *Discussing sports and hobbies (p. 51)*

1 Students can usefully work together on this. With weaker students it may be best to ask them to identify the three correct sentences first. If you have time, ask students to follow up on mistakes they missed by using the problem structure in true sentences about themselves.

When checking, you may want to draw students' attention to the following points:
1. *sport/s* (countable) a particular type of sport, e.g. *Football is one of the most popular sports.* *sport* (uncountable) sport in general, e.g. *Sport is good for your health.*
5. *Game* and *match* have the same meaning in British English (NB In American English *match* is only used to describe a competition between two people, not teams), e.g. *a wrestling match.* You can say either *a football game* or *a game of football* but you can only say *a football match* (not *a match of football*)
6. We use *sports* as an adjective before a noun, e.g. *sports shop, sports equipment*
10. We use the verb *go* with most sports ending in *-ing*. (e.g. swimming/jogging, etc.) (See Essential language)

2 Focus on the Essential language first, and make sure students can use the phrases appropriately and confidently. Practise, using a different topic such as holiday activities, and focus on stress and intonation if necessary. Monitor the pairwork and encourage students to develop each topic a little.

3 Again, draw students' attention to the Essential language first and provide practice if necessary, using different statements. Monitor discussions and, if pairwork begins to flag, you could move into an open class discussion. Give feedback afterwards on students' performances in relation to exam requirements, including plenty of emphasis on the positive!

Focus on reading 1 *The Boys of Summer, the Men of Fall (p. 52)*

1 Read through the Exam Link first and then allow a few moments for students to read and think about the title and sub-title. Ask for examples of a sport that even quite elderly people can do (e.g. golf, swimming) and one that only younger people can do well (e.g. gymnastics, high jump). Check understanding of *endurance* (the ability to continue doing something difficult or strenuous for a long time) but avoid explaining *component* or *deteriorate* at this stage as these feature in the next exercise.

2 Remind students of the importance of underlining key words in exam questions. Allow only a few moments for this task to emphasise that you can answer factual questions like this successfully without the need for slow, careful reading.

3 a) Be prepared to work through this introduction quite slowly as a class, if necessary, so that everyone is clear about it. b) Let students complete the matching task and compare answers. Clarify vocabulary as necessary.

4–6 Allow students to work through the three exam practice tasks at their own speed, monitoring progress as they work. NB Task 2 is designed to be an easy introduction to classification tasks. Let students compare answers and, when checking, make sure they can justify answers by reference to the text.

Focus on grammar *Present perfect (p. 54)*

The tasks in this section are designed as revision. If your students are less confident with basic grammar, you may need to provide extra support and a more step-by-step approach. You may also prefer lower level students to work through the section on the present perfect in the Key language bank (p. 151) before continuing.

Focus on reading 2 *The curse of the referee (p. 55)*

1 Discuss the questions as a class. Clarify *referee, umpire* and *judge* if necessary. While discussing ideas, elicit useful topic vocabulary such as *goal, net, court, ring, spectator, crowd*, etc.

2/3 Read through the Task Approach as a class and let students begin work on the task. It may be helpful to remind them that they need to look for parallel expressions (e.g. top = *highest*).

Stop them after 1–2 minutes and ask how much of the text they need to read in order to answer the question. If they can't answer, point out that this information is

given in the Tip box (lines 1–24 only). Make sure they've also taken note of the information in the first Tip box.

Use this to underline a key point: always read the instructions! However, it's important to explain that this information is not given in the exam. Ask:
- how they would know which section they need to read (by studying the questions).
- why it's important to know this in the exam (it saves reading time).

When checking, ask students to justify their answers by reference to the text.

4 Read through the Task Advice as a class and make sure students have noticed which part of the text they need to concentrate on. Give them time to highlight the sports A–H in the text and let them compare results or check as a class that they've done this correctly. Repeat this process for underlining key words in the questions. When checking, ask students to justify their answers by reference to the text.

Focus on speaking 2 *Describing a person (p. 57)*

1 If this game is new to students or you feel they need help with ideas for questions, you could demonstrate using a famous person (not a sports person) that they are all likely to have heard of, e.g. a current film star/a well-known head of state/a famous author from the past. Before beginning the activity, check that everyone understands the rules.

2 a) Before students study the task card, have a brief recap on the procedure in Part 2 of the interview (as described in the Exam Link on p. 30).
  b) Give students time to read through the instructions and then, while they're preparing, tour round to check on their choice of subject and mindplans.

3 Focus on the Essential language first and make sure students can use the expressions appropriately and confidently. Practise with a different subject, e.g. a member of your family that you admire, before returning to the sports topic for the exam practice. Monitor the pairwork and, if you have time, you could usefully extend the practice by asking students to describe people from the past, e.g. a historical figure, a teacher they have known.

IELTS Vocabulary Building *(p. 59)*

The exercises in this section can either be completed for homework or in class time.

Unit 5 Key

Lead-in (p. 50)
See Student's book p. 168

Focus on speaking 1 (p. 51)
1 1 <u>does</u> ... sports (especially British English) or
    <u>plays</u> ... <u>sport</u> (especially US English)
2   at ~~the~~ sport (uncountable noun in general)
3 game
4 ✓
5 a football match (British English) or a game of
    football
6 ✓
7 took <u>part</u> in
8 support (a permanent rather than a temporary
    situation)
9 ✓
10 <u>go</u> running ('go' is used with all sports ending in
    -ing, e.g. go swimming/jogging, etc. See Essential
    language box)

Focus on reading 1 (p. 52)
2 1 power, endurance, good nerves
2 weight-lifting, rowing or wrestling
3 gymnastics or field events (e.g. sprint, triple jump,
    hurdles)
4 oxygen
3a 1 Question 1 (*ingredients, excellence*)
2 Question 4 (*provides energy = fuels*)
3 Questions 2 and 3.
3b 1 f) 2 g) 3 c) 4 h) 5 b) 6 d) 7 a)
    8 e)
4 1 human movement
2 30
3 neurons (nerves)
5 1 B 2 C 3 A 4 B 5 A
6 1 F (They die off throughout life but this *makes
    little difference until the age of 50 or beyond*)
2 T (*Forty-year-old rowers ... remain competitive
    with 25-year-olds*)
3 NG
4 F (every <u>decade</u> after the age of 30)
5 T (*Ageing takes its biggest toll in the sprints and
    jumps ...*)

Focus on grammar (p. 54)
1 1 have found
2 have been here, have learnt, have made
3 has declared
The correct statements are:
1 A, C 2 A, B 3 B, C

2 *Example answers*
1 I've already eaten/I've just had lunch.
2 I've never been there.
3 He's just passed his driving test/qualified as a
    doctor, etc.
4 I haven't had/received/heard the results yet.
5 The check-in desk has just/already closed.
4 1 had to 2 supplied 3 were 4 has improved
5 used 6 made 7 has increased 8 played
9 has been 10 has become

Focus on reading 2 (p. 55)
3 1 verbal 2 pay 3 examinations 4 vision
5 fitness 6 regularly 7 especially
4 *Suggested answers*
Students may prefer to underline more or fewer
words – this is essentially a matter of personal
choice.
1 <u>give</u> <u>spectators</u> <u>reasons for</u> ... <u>decisions</u>
    (*Example*)
2 <u>weather conditions</u> ... <u>uncomfortable</u>.
3 <u>examine</u> ... <u>footwear</u>.
4 <u>injured</u> ... <u>heavy contestant</u>
5 <u>warn</u> <u>spectators</u> ... <u>behaviour</u>
6 <u>involved in the action</u> ... <u>prevent injury</u>
7 <u>difficult</u> ... <u>see</u> ... <u>rules</u> ... <u>broken</u>
Questions 1–7
1 C *explain ... decisions to the crowd (lines 51–52)*
2 A *stand for hours in blazing sunshine (27)*
3 E *The use of talcum powder on the soles of the
    shoes ... is forbidden (57–60)*
4 H *get crushed underneath a 300 kg man mountain
    (65–68)*
5 B *issue ... warnings against the use of mobile
    phones or flash photography by spectators
    (45–46)*
6 F *to protect the losing fighter from further
    punishment ... throw himself into the fight
    (62–65)*
7 D *75% of fouls are committed under water
    (53–55)*

IELTS Vocabulary Builder (p. 59)
1 1 compete; train
2 amateur; professional
3 record; goals
4 spectators; supporters; teams; stadium
5 pool; course; court
6 coach; event
2 1 do 2 play 3 go 4 do/play 5 do 6 go
4 Oo: umpire athlete football contest
oOo: athletics, supporter, spectator, gymnastics
ooO: referee, disappear, understand, entertain

6 ▶ Animal rights and wrongs

To set the ball rolling ...

Introduce the subject and elicit possible topic areas for speaking or writing, building up a mindplan on the board as you go and adding any useful topic vocabulary that emerges. It's also useful to gauge students' general attitude to animals/pets at this stage.

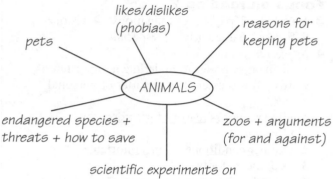

Lead-in (p. 60)

1 This works well as a pair discussion. Before students start, you could draw their attention to the expressions in question 1: to **keep** a pet (= own and look after); 2: to think **of** something (i.e. to consider in a particular way) v to think **about** something (= use your mind); 3: to **lead a** quiet/busy/exciting/stressful etc. **life**.

Monitor the pairwork and note other useful expressions to focus on afterwards, e.g: **for** company/protection; to spoil (v); spoilt (adj); to **over**eat; **over**feed (v); **over**fed (adj), etc. It is also an opportunity to revise the word 'substitute' which was introduced in Academic Word Study 1 (p. 26), e.g. **as a substitute for** children.

2 This exercise checks some basic topic vocabulary and gives students the chance to ask about other related words if they wish. Check what the words have in common as well as what the odd man out is, and why. There may well be other possible answers beyond the most obvious one, and these are perfectly acceptable as long as students can give good reasons. If you have time, you could extend the exercise with a few more groups or words.

Focus on speaking 1 *Discussing animals (p. 60)*

Focus on the Essential language first and clarify the difference between adjectives like *annoying* or *noisy* which are **gradeable,** and adjectives like *disgusting* which are **ungradeable.** Ungradeable adjectives either express extreme qualities like *furious*, or *exhausted* or absolute qualities like *true* or *dead.* They can only be used with a few intensifiers like *totally, absolutely* or *completely.* Gradeable adjectives can be used with a whole range of intensifiers including *very, slightly, quite, extremely,* etc.

It's worth practising this language briefly by asking a few questions (not related to animals!) *What do you think of Chinese food/ English TV programmes? How would you feel about eating insects?* etc. Encourage students to use a wider range of adjectives than those in the box and point out that the expression can also be used in the past: *What did you think of last night's football match?*

1 Check the instructions and demonstrate briefly how a conversation can be built by doing a mini interview on a slightly different topic. NB With reasonably able students, this could be treated more formally as exam practice for Part 1 of the Interview, if appropriate. Monitor students' conversations and, if not treated as exam practice, supply language as necessary, e.g. *My favourite animal is ..., I'm afraid I'm not an/a great animal lover (*NB similar expressions such as *a music lover, a nature lover, an art lover), I used to keep fish,* etc.

2 1 You could begin by telling students that half the households in the UK own a pet of some kind (or get them to guess). Then let them discuss the question briefly before supplying the answer (See Key).

2 Ask students to read through the instructions and list of people and then remind them about **depend on/depend if** (See Essential language, p. 34). Allow a reasonable time for this discussion and again note down useful language, e.g. **keep** a person **active, need** a lot of **attention,** teach a child about **responsibility,** etc.

Focus on grammar *Review of the present tenses (p. 61)*

The tasks in this section are designed as revision. If your students are less confident with basic grammar, you may need to provide extra support and a more step-by-step approach. You may also prefer lower level students to work through the sections on the present progressive and present simple in the Key language bank (pp. 152, 153) before continuing.

Read through the Exam Link and reinforce the message about the importance of the present tenses in the IELTS test. You could also see if students remember what percentage of English communication is based on present and past tenses (see Exam Link, p. 7).

Point out that even though students are likely to have 'done the present' many times before, they probably still make quite a few basic mistakes. The aim in looking at this area of language again is to become as **accurate as possible**. One way of doing this is for students to identify their most frequent mistakes. They can then check their work for these specific mistakes and hopefully eliminate most of them before they reach the teacher or examiner. NB Learning from mistakes is covered in the DIY section on p. 110 and there is no reason not to look at this now if you feel it would be helpful.

1 It may help to do the first question as an example. In this case, ask students which words in the correct extract (C) matched 'criminal' in the question (*prisoner, kidnapper, murderer*). Establish the gist of each extract before proceeding.

Let students compare answers before checking and discussing vocabulary clues. The extracts raise various interesting points and, if you have time, you could discuss one or more of these.

2 Make sure students are completely clear about what's required here. You may find with lower level students that it's best to work through the task together, telling them which extract to study in each case.

Optional Practice
Include this task if you think students would benefit from more oral practice. Give them a few minutes' thinking time and then let them compare answers in pairs.

1 things which are *happening now*. **Say three things that you are doing to achieve a specific goal.**
Examples: I'm saving up for a holiday. I'm trying to stop smoking.
2 **things which are *changing or developing*.** Say three things that are different in the way you learn or use English now, compared with the past.
Examples: I'm getting higher marks. I'm beginning to understand English humour.

3 Focus on the Essential language first, and ensure that students can use the phrases appropriately and confidently. If necessary practise with objects drawn on the board, e.g.
- a ruler: 30cm (L) x 3 cm (W)
- an elephant: 3 m (H) x 5 m (L) x 5 tons (W)
- The Eiffel Tower: 321 m (H) x 8,619 tons (W)
- (and if you want to introduce 'depth') The Grand Canyon: 1,600 m (D)

Let students study the two data sheets and clarify vocabulary as necessary, e.g. *habitat, status, threats, declining, clearance, swampy, poaching* (NB this was included in the Odd Man Out exercise on p. 60). Check answers for the gapped text carefully, highlighting the use of the present simple for basic facts about the animal (e.g. *lives in the forests*), and the present progressive for any condition which is now changing (e.g. *are currently declining*).

Depending on your students' ability, they may need to follow the model of the gorilla description fairly closely or they may be able to improvise around this general pattern.

Focus on listening 1 *Wildlife Film Festival (p. 63)*

1 Give students time to look through the numbers briefly before hearing the recording and to compare answers afterwards. Use the correction phase for oral practice.

2 When checking, add in any additional numbers, fractions, etc. that you feel might be useful.

3 As students should be familiar with most of these abbreviations the point of the exercise is mainly awareness-raising and confidence-building. Let them work through the list quickly in pairs and then focus on any which may be unfamiliar.

4 Give students time to study the task and answer the pre-questions a)–c). Encourage a few guesses for question c) but it's best not to force the issue if none are forthcoming. Play the recording once only and ask students to compare answers before checking.

DIY Learning Strategy *Make a note of it (p. 64)*

This section encourages students to record useful language in the most effective way for learning. This involves including as much relevant information as possible, and also setting words out in the most appropriate way, which may be in the form of a diagram.

You could begin by asking students to find an example of vocabulary they have recorded recently and to explain one of the items to their partner. Afterwards discuss results: How well did they remember the meaning? Would they be confident enough to use the word? Would they know how to pronounce it? How much do they know about the word, e.g. what words it can combine with?, etc.

Move on to analysing the examples A–E. Discuss the advantages of each one and also the <u>kind</u> of expressions it would be useful to record in that way. Make it clear that this is a question of 'horses for courses': different approaches suit different kinds of language.

Let students read through the rules and, if possible, illustrate detailed examples.

For the DIY Learning project, discuss suitable places for students to keep a permanent record of useful language and check that they realise they have to try at least one new way of recording vocabulary. They will benefit from encouragement and positive feedback so agree a date when you will check the new improved records (and put it in your diary!)

Focus on speaking 2 *Discussing moral issues (p. 64)*

This small section includes several big topics, so allow plenty of time – anything from 15 to 30 minutes – to cover them. There are various ways of handling the discussion but as a suggestion, divide the questions into two sections. For questions 1 and 2, ask students to take turns interviewing each other, and to give as detailed answers as possible. Monitor their discussions and note down useful language to focus on later. At an appropriate point, interrupt and invite feedback. For questions 3 and 4, tell students to discuss the issues and try to reach agreement. Again monitor the discussions and give appropriate feedback.

Focus on listening 2 *The right to roam (p. 65)*

After students have had time to read through the instructions and questions, ask what kind of answer they'd expect for question 1 (e.g. the name of a university or research institute) and invite ideas for question 3. It's worth making sure that students can 'read' the table with a few check questions, e.g. *How many animals are included in the table? What's the difference between the two on the left and the two on the right? What information do you need for Q 5, etc.* Clarify *infant mortality rate* and invite a few guesses for Qs 6 and 8.

Note that the table in this listening task provides the basis for Task 1 writing practice describing this table in the Writing practice bank (p. 159) There is a gapped model answer with focus questions on key language features.

Focus on grammar 2 *Comparison (p. 66)*

1 Students have probably covered this language area before, perhaps several times, but it's likely that they still make mistakes with it. Given the importance of comparison, particularly in Task 1 of the Writing paper, it's well worth aiming to clear up the main areas of confusion.

This task is designed as revision. If your students are less confident with basic grammar, you may need to provide extra support and a more step-by-step approach. It may also be helpful for lower level students to work through the section on comparatives and superlatives in the Key language bank (p. 142) before continuing.

Read through the Exam Link and go over the two structures and examples as systematically as you feel necessary. Ask students to suggest a few more examples based on the bar graph, prompting if required e.g.
Compare mammals and reptiles using *more.*
Compare fish and birds using *as.*
Tell me about birds using *the least endangered,* etc.

2/3/4 Check vocabulary as necessary e.g. *venomous.* Let students discuss and answer questions in pairs or, if time is short, go through them as a class.

5 Take the first sentence as an example, and elicit suitable adjectives (*noisiest/ loudest*) so that it's clear to students that they need to choose a suitable adjective for the context.

6 a) One member of the pair could select an adjective for their partner to use in a sentence. You could also extend this activity to include superlatives. It would be useful if students put one or two examples in writing after brief oral practice, so that you have a chance to monitor their work.
b) This could usefully be treated as exam practice for Section 2 of the Interview. In this case, give students a minute or so to prepare and encourage them to make notes, perhaps in the form of a mindplan.

Optional Additional practice
If you have time, you may want to focus on two useful expressions.

- **more or less** meaning 'almost'. It's fairly informal and is mostly used in speaking.

e.g. *The course is **more or less** finished now - there are only two evenings to go. It's **more or less** certain that there will be an election in May.*

Ask students to use the phrase ***more or less*** in true sentences of their own.

- **at least** expresses a minimum number or amount, e.g. *It takes **at least** an hour to prepare. I've got **at least** two major complaints.*

  Ask students to answer the following questions using ***at least.***

  How long do you spend studying in the evening?
  How many weeks' holiday a year do you think people should have?
  How often do you speak to, or contact, your best friend?

Focus on writing *Task 2: Presenting and justifying an opinion (p. 67)*

Let students read through the writing topic and then ask them to suggest what the four stages of tackling a Task 2 writing task would be. They can check by looking at the four margin headings in this section. Run through each stage before continuing:

1 **Analyse the question** This is crucial. Tell them how easy it is to lose marks by not thinking carefully enough about the question.
2 **Plan your answer** Point out how important it is to spend a few moments deciding on the best way to organise their essay and thinking of different arguments.
3 **Write your answer** This will be much easier when it is based on a logical plan.
4 **Check your answer** They'll say there isn't time for this but point out that even one or two minutes is enough to spot a couple of their favourite grammar or spelling mistakes.

1 These questions could usefully be discussed in pairs. When checking answers, encourage general discussion and note relevant topic vocabulary that comes up.

Before students turn over the page and see the example plan, establish the (minimum) four sections for addressing a typical **For/Against** topic (1 Introduction; 2 Arguments for; 3 Arguments against; 4 Conclusion), and perhaps elicit some preliminary ideas for the **For/Against** columns.

2 Once students have read through the plan, check understanding and clarify vocabulary as necessary. Allow time for them to discuss ideas in pairs and then open a class discussion, again noting useful language.

Ask how many arguments **For** and **Against** they need to include in an exam essay. Then ask them to pick the two from each column which they feel are most important. They should also think about the best way to begin and end the essay.

NB It's a good idea to ask how many words there should be in each of the four sections as a way of underlining the need to keep an overall balance. A reasonable (and easy to remember) suggestion would be to allow one third of the total number of words (i.e. about 85) for the introduction and conclusion combined, one third for the arguments FOR and one third for the arguments AGAINST. This matches the gapped model answer.

3 Check answers for the gapped introductory section and then allow time for students to complete the other three sections, either in class or for homework, as appropriate.

Note that there is a model answer for this task in the Writing practice bank (p. 159), with questions focusing on key features of organisation and language.

IELTS Vocabulary Building *(p. 69)*

The exercises in this section can either be completed for homework or in class time.

Optional pronunciation practice

1 Explain that the plural ending -*(e)s* or can be pronounced in three ways in English (see below) and practise as necessary.

/s/ as in *hiss*   /z/ as in *buzz*   /ɪz/ as in *buzzes*

2 Ask students to look at the word groups below and say which word in each group has the sound /z/.

mouse house blouse
horse cause course
goose loose choose

3 Ask students to say which of the sounds: /s/, /ɪz/ or /z/ comes at the end of each of the following words.

a) baskets   e) horses   i) stables
b) bees   f) kennels   j) wings
c) cages   g) nests
d) cats   h) snakes

Answers
2 blouse, cause, choose
3 a) /s/ b) /z/ c) /ɪz/ d) /s/ e) /ɪz/ f) /z/ g) /s/
h) /s/ i) /z/ j) /z/

Unit 6 Key

Lead-in (p. 60)

1 *Example answers*

1 People generally keep pets for company/companionship but also for protection.
2 Some people think of their pets as (substitute) children.
3 Some pets are spoilt, e.g. overfed; others are kept like prisoners.

2 *Suggested answers*

1 **wolf** – not a domestic animal
2 **botanist** – the others study or work with animals in their jobs, a botanist studies plants
3 **nest** – the only natural animal home
4 **bat** – not an insect
5 **breeding** – the others are ways of killing animals

Focus on speaking 1 (p. 60)

2 1 The most popular pets in the UK are:
Fish (25 million); Cat (7.7 million);
Dog (6.7 million); Bird (2.3 million);
Rabbit (1.5 million)

Focus on grammar 1 (p. 61)

1 1 C 2 E 3 B 4 A 5 D

2 *Example answers*

2 Extract E: <u>lowers</u> your heart rate…; <u>makes</u> you more relaxed
3 Extract B Dogs <u>see</u> us …, we <u>think</u> …;
Extract D: he <u>loves</u> you, He <u>needs</u> you,
4 Extract A: We <u>are keeping</u> more pets …; The number … <u>is increasing</u>
Extract C: Pets <u>are helping</u> …; Inmates <u>are forming</u> bonds …

3 *Example answers*

The Lowland gorilla … and eats a diet of <u>leaves</u>. It has a height of <u>(up to) 175 cm</u> and males weigh between <u>135</u> and <u>275</u> kg. Numbers are currently declining as a result of <u>forest clearance</u>.

The Greater one-horned rhinoceros lives on grasslands in swampy areas in NE India and Nepal, and **eats** a diet of (principally/mainly) grass. It **has a length of** 412 cm and **weighs** up to 2000kg. The rhinoceros is endangered **because of/as a result** of habitat loss and poaching but numbers **are** now **increasing following/as a result** of intensive conservation programmes.

Focus on listening 1 (p. 63)

1 1 B 2 A 3 C 4 B 5 C

3 1 morning
2 arrive
3 degrees
4 number (mainly US)
5 Telephone
6 maximum
7 minutes
8 kilometres per hour
9 number
10 depart
11 square metre
12 percentage

3 Exam practice
a) 1, 6, 7, 10 **b)** 3, 8
1 10.30 a.m. 2 food 3 Japan 4 Ocean
5 scientists 6 10/ten years 7 1500 8 UK
9 Behaviour 10 973 4617

DIY Learning strategy (p. 64)

Example answers

A A diagram like this (sometimes called a spidergram) is a good way of organising and learning a range of topic vocabulary.
B Giving a brief example of the new word in context makes it easier to remember the meaning and use. It's often important to record the pronunciation, and phonemic symbols are the most reliable way of doing this. It's worth learning to recognise phonemic symbols because they are used in most good dictionaries.
C Learning words with other members of their 'word families' (e.g. noun, verb, adjective) is an efficient way of learning vocabulary.
D With some vocabulary, a diagram is the most effective way of showing meaning.
E It's very helpful to learn a word with its common 'word partners', so that you know which words it can combine with and which it can't.

Focus on listening 2 (p. 65)

1 Oxford University
2 *Nature*
3 stress
4 Lion
5 79,000
6 minimum
7 .5
8 (in) a/each/per day
9 1.5
10 14.3

Focus on grammar 2 *(p. 66)*

1 *Example answers*

Reptiles are less endangered than mammals.
Amphibians are more endangered than birds and reptiles.
Reptiles are not so endangered as mammals.

2 1 the largest *Answer:* Blue whale (34m long)
2 the fastest *Answer:* Cheetah (105 km/h)
3 the most venomous *Answer:* Snake (The venom of one Australian taipan snake could kill 125,000 mice.)
4 the best *Answer:* Large birds of prey (e.g. eagle) (It has been calculated that some species can see three or more times further than humans)
5 Students' own ideas

3 more successfully, most severely

4 *Example answers*

1 large, (larger) largest
2 (happy) happier, (happiest)
3 more endangered, most venomous, more successfully, most severely
4 better, best
5 worse, worst
6 less, least
7 more, most

5 *Suggested answers*

1 the noisiest
2 The most dangerous /ferocious/aggressive, etc.
3 The highest/greatest
4 heaviest/largest
5 most intelligent

Focus on writing *(p. 68)*

3 1 concerned, sad, etc
2 move (freely)/run/roam about/hunt
3 in zoos/in captivity
4 However
5 sides

See model answer in Writing bank p. 159

IELTS Vocabulary Builder *(p. 69)*

1 1 on 2 for 3 from 4 between; on 5 for
6 of; after 7 at 8 as

2 a) captivity (also *capture*, 'the act of capturing')
b) captive
c) behaviour
d) extinct
e) conservation
f) zoological
g) migration (also *migrant*, a person who migrates)
h) migratory
i) enclosure
j) enclosed
k) survival (also *survivor*, a person who survives)

3 1 speak 2 listen to 3 see 4 tell 5 prevented

7 ▶ Appropriate technology

To set the ball rolling ...

Ask students to suggest a few key technological inventions, modern or historical. Choose one or two and discuss why they were important and what life now would be like without them. If students are short of inspiration, you could supply a few ideas, e.g. accurate clocks (C17), trains (C18), refrigerator (1913), credit cards (1951),

You could also adapt this phase into a game, if you have time. Put students in small groups and allot each person an invention (see suggestions below). He or she then has to use their imagination and powers of persuasion to argue the case for the importance of their invention. The group can vote on the 'winner'.

> e.g. the electric food mixer (1945), Scotch cellophane tape (1920), the dishwasher (1885, surprisingly), sunglasses (C18), binoculars (1823), wristwatches (C19), tinned food (C19), blue jeans (1873).

Lead-in *(p. 72)*

1 With books closed, explain the newspaper survey and invite students to guess the readers' top choice. Then let them study the instructions, inventions and pie chart. Clarify *vaccination* if necessary (*vaccine* = a weak form of the bacteria or virus which causes a disease. *Vaccination* = putting a vaccine into a person's body as a way of protecting them from a disease) and check pronunciation: i.e. vaccine Oo, vaccination ooOo.

Ask students to discuss ideas in pairs and try to reach agreement. Monitor the discussions and afterwards invite one or two pairs to explain their decisions.

2 The following language is useful for expressing reactions, and it might be appropriate to introduce and practise it here before inviting students' comments on the actual results of the survey. With lower level students it may be best to stick to the spoken language examples to avoid confusion between *surprised/surprising*. With stronger students you could make a teaching point of this and include *interested/interesting, bored/boring* as well.

> ### Useful Language
> #### Spoken English
> **I'm not surprised** (that) …
> **I'm** (quite/really) **surprised** (that) …
> **I can't believe** (that) …
> #### Written English
> **It's surprising/not surprising** (that) …
> **It's interesting/amazing/astonishing** (that) …

3 Give students time to discuss these points in pairs and then invite feedback, focusing particularly on the third, which links to the topics of the reading texts.

If time allows, you could extend the discussion on this topic in various ways, for example by giving students a different top ten (there are many on the Internet) and letting them comment on it, using expressions from the Useful language box above. They could also choose items to make up their own top five inventions.

Focus on reading 1 *Changing lives* *(p. 72)*

1 Give students a few moments to study the pictures and then elicit ideas as to why each invention might be needed, taking the opportunity to input relevant language. Accept all logical answers without identifying the correct one.

2 Read through the Exam Link and check that students remember what 'skimming' is (see p. 8). Set a time limit to prevent students from reading in too much detail. When checking, ask them to mention any clues that helped identify each topic. Make sure everyone has written the name of the correct invention by each text before continuing.

3 Check that students remember what 'scanning' is (see p. 8) and remind them of the speed element. Monitor progress on exercises 1 and 2, assisting as necessary.

In exercise 2 you may need to clarify some vocabulary in the questions, e.g. *capacity, estimated, proportion,* but delay explaining *malnourished/malnourishment* (when checking, point out that it is possible to answer question 2 d) correctly without understanding these words). It may also help lower level students if they write the letter of the relevant text after each question before they start.

4 *Questions 1–4* (Sentence completion)
Read through the Exam Link and then ask students to study questions 1 to 4. Check what reading skills they expect to use (scanning) and encourage them to answer the questions as quickly as possible.

Questions 5–10 (Matching)
Read through the Task Approach as a class, and then focus on the example. Agree the parts which need underlining ('blue cloth' and 'construction') and ask students to find the place in text B where the necessary information is given. Establish that the phrase which matches 'construction' is *They are built using* ....

Give students time to underline the other key words and phrases, and check results briefly. Ask them to write the expressions from the text which match the parts they've underlined, next to each question. Finally, ask if they need to answer questions in order or not (just checking!). Afterwards check answers and reasons thoroughly.

Questions 11–15 (Labelling a diagram)
Read through the Task Approach as a class. With lower level students, establish that everyone has located the part of the text where the fish cage is described before they begin. Monitor carefully, and encourage students to compare and discuss answers as they go along.

Focus on grammar *Passive (p. 77)*

The tasks in this section are designed as revision. If your students are less confident with basic grammar, you may need to provide extra support and a more step-by-step approach. You may also prefer lower level students to work through the section on the passive in the Key language bank (p. 148) before continuing.

Focus on reading 2 *The price is wrong (p. 78)*

Questions 1–5
Students should be able to complete the guidelines fairly easily but it's important that they are aware of the reasons for the advice, so ask why in each case and refer them back to the relevant page if necessary.

- Underlining key words and phrases, Exam Link p. 31
- Using the first one or two sentences to identify the topic of a paragraph, instructions for task 2, p. 73
- Skimming skills, Exam Link p. 73 (and elsewhere)

Let students complete the task, reminding them to leave more difficult questions till last if necessary, and compare answers before checking.

Questions 6–10
Let students underline key expressions in pairs. Remind them that with matching questions like this the items to choose from will always be listed in the order that they appear in the text (See Tip, p. 97). This is quite a dense text so it's best to monitor progress fairly carefully in order to steer less able students in the right direction and generally assist and encourage. When checking, ask students to quote from the text to justify their answers.

Question 11 (Multiple choice)
Point out that in a multiple choice question all the options are designed to look possible and it's only by studying the text very carefully that you can decide which one is correct. You could check understanding of 'genetically modified crops' if you wish but students should be able to answer the question correctly without knowing this term, and encouraging this leap of faith is valuable exam training. Discuss the clues to the answer: *the report backs* ... and *to reject GM crops is to give up a huge opportunity* ... allow us to ignore answers A and B and concentrate on C and D. The last sentence pinpoints the correct answer C.

Focus on speaking *Describing places (p. 80)*

Optional introductory activity
Remind students that the inventions in *Focus on reading 1* of this unit come from the four countries: Bangladesh, Cambodia, Kenya, and Nepal, and ask if they can tell you anything about them. Don't worry (or be surprised) if they can't! Next show them the following descriptions on a handout or overhead transparency and ask them to match each to one of the four countries. Check answers and clarify useful topic vocabulary such as *land-locked, flooded, vital, devastated*.

a) This is a mountainous and completely land-locked country. It is the only Hindu state in the world.
b) This is a low, flat land, which is regularly flooded during the annual monsoon. It is the world's most densely populated country.
c) This country is situated on the Equator. Tourism is vital to the economy, and the country offers both wildlife safaris and beach holidays.
d) This country suffered two decades of civil war during the last century, which devastated the economy.

You could also draw students' attention to the use of **non-defining relative clauses** in the texts, as follows. There is more information on this language area in the Key language bank (p. 155).

Ask students to underline the two clauses beginning 'which' in b) and d) and explain that these are called **non-defining (ND) relative clauses.** Ask:

* If you took away the ND relative clause, would the sentence still make sense? (Yes)
* Could you leave out the word *which,* or use the word *that* instead? (No)
* Is it necessary to put a comma before a ND relative clause? (Yes)

1 Check that students remember the procedure for Part 2 of the interview and give them time to study the question and decide on a place to describe.

2 This task highlights the fact that a mindplan needs to match the specific points on the topic card, and it's worth making this explicit. Once students have drafted their mindplan, they should check it against the topic card to make sure they've included all the key points with no unnecessary extras. Discuss the questions but allow flexibility with regard to 2 and 3, which are more subjective.

Focus on the Essential language and check any vocabulary students are unsure of. If your students need extra

practice in this important language area, use photocopied maps, ideally with topographical features like mountains and deserts marked, or use invented countries. Then ask students to work in pairs and make as many true sentences as possible about their own countries, using expressions from the box.

Finally ask students to describe their chosen place, working in pairs. They should try to speak for about two minutes. After that their partner can ask one or two questions to round off.

Note that there is additional Task 1 writing practice on the topic of climate in the Writing practice bank (p. 160). This has an Essential language box for describing graphs, which would be useful to focus on in class, and guided tasks which are suitable for homework.

IELTS Vocabulary Building
(p. 81)

The exercises in this section can either be completed for homework or in class time.

Unit 7 Key

Lead-in *(p. 72)*
See Student's book p. 168
3 vaccination, 1796. The other dates are: electricity 1831, bicycle 1885, computer 1936, World Wide Web 1991

Focus on reading 1 *(p. 72)*
2 A Bicycle ambulance
  B Tsetse fly trap
  C Fish cage
  D Wooden wheelchair
3 1

a)	£40
b)	£5
c)	£150
d)	£20

  2 a) More than 800 (D)
    b) One cubic metre (up to 300 fish) (C)
    c) 500,000 (B)
    d) 56 per cent/% (C)
    e) 12 months/1 year (D)
Questions 1–4
  1 plains (A)
  2 sleeping sickness (B)
  3 'hapa' (C)
  4 (the) Mekong (D)

Questions 5–10
  5 D … takes <u>approximately two hours</u> to <u>assemble</u>
  6 A *The charity …was already working with villagers to build bicycle trailers … the next step was <u>to adapt</u> them to become ambulances.*
  7 C … <u>scraps and waste;</u> … <u>kitchen waste</u>
  8 D …*packs flat … <u>making transport of the vehicle very efficient</u>.*
  9 B … <u>a single trap is ineffective</u> … *it's important that farmers build <u>a number of traps</u> across an area.*
  10 A <u>*In response to user comments, a cover*</u> has been designed that can be added …
Questions 11–15
11 Bamboo poles
12 String
13 Floats
14 Cotton
15 Moulded metal

Focus on grammar *(p. 77)*
1 *Example answers*
  1 The two-wheel trailer <u>is made</u> from moulded metal … (A); people <u>are</u> also <u>affected</u> by the disease … (B); …these <u>are secured</u> with string. (C); thousands <u>are disabled</u> by mines … (D)
  2 the charity Motivation <u>was asked</u> to address … (D)

3 a cover <u>has been designed</u> … (A)
4 Past perfect
5 had been
6 Future
7 will be
8 The bed section <u>can be padded</u> … (A)

3 1 False 2 True 3 True 4 False
5 False (modals can also be used)

4 *Example answers*
1 Tickets are sold at/can be obtained from the box office.
2 The exam results will be announced in August.
3 The election was won by the communists.
4 The latest information can be downloaded from the Internet.
5 A new species of spider has been discovered.
6 No sharp objects must be carried in your hand luggage.

Focus on reading 2 *(p. 78)*

Task Approach
underline/highlight
first
skimming

Questions 1–5
1 C **2** E **3** D **4** F **5** B

Questions 6–10
6 Sub-Saharan Africa (*Para. F*) *Time has stood still in many areas such as Sub-Saharan Africa …*
7 Kenya (*C*)
8 Bangladesh (*A*) *cheap oral-rehydration therapy … has dramatically cut the death toll from childhood diarrhoea*
9 Brazil (*F*)
10 South Africa (*E*)

Question 11
11 C (*F*) the report backs genetically modified crops …

Focus on speaking *(p. 80)*

1 Main cities, Geography, Climate, Tourist attractions
2 *Suggested answer* Government, Natural resources
3 *Suggested answer* Location, People

IELTS Vocabulary Builder *(p. 81)*

1 **Climate/Weather**: cyclone, drought, flooding, humidity, monsoon, showers
Geography: bay, coastline, estuary, forest, plain, valley
Natural resources: mineral deposit, natural gas, oil reserves, rubber, timber, water

2 1 agricultu**ral** 2 **urban** 3 coast**al** 4 **rural**
5 forest**ed** 6 hill**y** 7 industri**al** 8 marshy
9 mountain**ous**

3 grow /grəʊ/, tough /tʌf/

4 cough /kɒf/, though /θəʊ/

8 ▶ Communications

To set the ball rolling ...

Introduce the subject and elicit possible topic areas for speaking or writing, building up a mindplan on the board as you go.

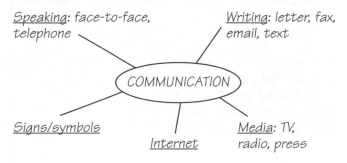

Speaking: face-to-face, telephone

Writing: letter, fax, email, text

COMMUNICATION

Signs/symbols

Internet

Media: TV, radio, press

Lead-in (p. 82)

1 Monitor discussions and use the feedback stage as an opportunity to input additional relevant language.

2 After the pairwork, open a more general discussion about variations in the meanings of signs or symbols in different cultures, such as the significance of certain **colours** (e.g. white associated with weddings in some countries but with mourning and funerals in others) or particular **hand signals** (e.g. a thumbs up sign meaning 'OK' in the USA and much of Europe, but indicating number 1 in Germany and number 5 in Japan!). This leads appropriately into the next question.

3 Encourage students to make brief notes so that they can report back on their conversations. Remind them if necessary about useful language for speculating (see Essential language p. 28).

Focus on grammar *Permission, prohibition and obligation (p. 83)*

The tasks in this section are designed as revision. If your students are less confident with basic grammar, you may need to provide extra support and a more step-by-step approach. You may also prefer lower level students to work through the section on modal verbs in the Key language bank (p. 146) before continuing.

1 Read through the Exam Link as a class. Give students time to study the table and check understanding of vocabulary as necessary. e.g. 'Is it compulsory to wear a crash helmet in <u>your</u> country?'

2 Let students work together to identify and correct the mistakes.

3 Point out that they can find all the answers by studying the table in Exercise 1 and the corrected sentences in Exercise 2. Check and/or clarify understanding of these rules.

4 Introduce this section using a different topic such as 'driving on a motorway', and give a few prompts e.g. **keep to the speed limit** (*You must/have to ...*); **park your car and have a picnic** (*You can't ...*); **overtake** (*You're allowed to ...*). You could also use **ride a bicycle/use your mobile phone/hitchhike**, etc. although these will elicit different answers according to the country students come from.

When checking, you could extend the discussion of the first point, a subject which students usually find fascinating! Encourage them to talk about the questions below in relation to their own country and explain some of the conventions in your country.
- Can you arrive early? How late can you arrive?
- Do you have to take a gift? If so, what is suitable?
- What if you don't like the food – can you refuse it?
- Can you ask for more food?
- Do you have to finish all the food on your plate?

5 Whether students complete this exercise in class or for homework, check the results carefully. If you think students would benefit from more written practice, ask them to put a few examples from each question in exercise 4 in writing as well.

Focus on listening 1 *Mobile phone safety (p. 84)*

Take the task in two parts. Allow time for students to look through each set of questions in advance and check that they can 'read' the pie charts by asking a few check questions, e.g. Which colour section, blue or red, do you need to look at? How do you know? What percentage does each diagram represent? Check that they remember why thinking about possible answers in advance is helpful (See Exam Link p. 43).

You may need to clarify some of the vocabulary in questions 4–10, especially with lower level students (e.g. *on standby, emissions, aerial, reception, gadgets*). You could also invite ideas about possible answers for some of the questions. When checking, remind them that correct spelling is essential (e.g. *week/weak*).

Focus on speaking 1 *Discussing communications (p. 85)*

1 You may prefer to deal with question 4 separately, in which case ask students to work through questions 1–3 only. Introduce the activity by giving a brief example to show the kind of supplementary questions that can be asked, and circulate during pairwork to encourage mini conversations. Afterwards invite students to report back on what their partner has told them, mentioning the reasons he or she gave. For question 4, check that students understand the question, and after the discussion, invite feedback. Let them check the result of the survey and remind them of the useful language for expressing a reaction (see p. 32 in this book).

2 Read through the Exam Link and ask students to say which tenses would be involved in answering each question. Then go through the Essential language as a class, focusing on the three main structures illustrated: **used to** + infinitive; **past simple**; **remember** + *-ing*. Practise each one as necessary using a different topic, e.g. What have been the main changes in, e.g. entertainment/transport/music?

For the interview phase, encourage a degree of formality by asking students to sit facing each other. Allow 4–5 minutes for each 'interview', as in the exam, and monitor progress. Give feedback on students' performances in relation to exam criteria.

Focus on writing 1 *Task 1: Describing a diagram (p. 86)*

1 Let students answer the questions individually and then compare answers.

2 Remind students how important it is to **select** key information and explain that an answer which describes a lot of random points will not score high marks. Reinforce this message by asking them to cover the questions while they study diagram A and decide on three important things to say about it. Let them compare ideas and invite feedback before they answer questions 1–3.

3 Let students compare answers before checking. To maximise practice of the target language, insist that they give full correct answers.

4 Focus on the Essential language first, and make sure students can use the expressions confidently before continuing. If you feel they would benefit from more practice of this important language, ask them to write a few correct sentences describing diagrams A and B. Alternatively, provide some different, simpler, data for

them to describe.

Ask students to write their sentences on a piece of paper which can be passed to another student easily. It's important to monitor the sentences they prepare as far as possible, to avoid them working with too many errors in the next phase. With less able students you could make this a pairwork activity to provide more support.

5 Read through the Exam Link and check that students are clear about this important point. Study the first part of the question, making sure students understand how the examples are set out, with the original wording on the left and suggested ways of rephrasing the information on the right. They may find questions a)–d) easier to answer if they work in pairs.

6 Read through the Essential language and point out that as this is appropriate for ninety per cent of all data-based Task 1 topics, it is a highly predictable element and is therefore well worth preparing in advance! Ideally let students complete this task in class, where you can monitor and guide. If time is short, at least let students answer questions 1–3 and check in class before they complete the paragraph for homework.

Focus on speaking 2 *Internet activities (p. 88)*

1 Suggest that students approach the task from the point of view of young people like themselves, but also consider the interests of older people, like their parents (or grandparents). Encourage them to use the language of speculation (see Essential language p. 28). Let them check the result of the survey and remind them of the useful language for expressing a reaction (see p. 32 in this book).

Exam practice
To give students a more realistic exam experience, let one 'candidate' work through both Parts 1 and 2, before swapping roles with his/her partner. Monitor the interviews and note key points for general feedback at the end. Begin by organising students into pairs with a designated examiner and candidate and rearranging seating as far as possible so students can face each other exam-style.

Briefly demonstrate how the first prompt in Part 1 can be turned into a question. With less able students you may need to run through all the questions in this way. You could also demonstrate an unsatisfactory, monosyllabic answer as a way of reminding students they need to give as full answers as possible.

Remind 'examiners' to keep an eye on timing for Part 2, allowing about one minute for preparation and two minutes speaking time, before asking one or two closing questions. Finish with a round-up of exam-focused feedback.

Focus on writing 2 *Task 2: Presenting and justifying an opinion (p. 89)*

1 Establish the four stages (to match the four margin headings on p. 68), and make sure students complete the table correctly. Read through the Exam Link as a class and ask how long they think they should spend on each of the four stages. The point is not to establish a hard and fast rule but to make students aware of time constraints and the importance of time management.

2 Let students work through the section in pairs before opening up a class discussion, taking the opportunity to input additional relevant language.

3 Once students have decided on the four sections, ask them to work together to jot down ideas for each section on a larger piece of paper. Have a class round-up of ideas and input useful vocabulary.

4 The writing task is suitable for timed exam practice in class (allow 30–35 minutes writing/checking time).

Note that there is a useful task focusing on the selection of relevant ideas for Task 2 topics in the **Writing practice bank** on p. 162. This works well as a class discussion.

Focus on listening 2 *Txt don't talk (p. 90)*

Questions 1–4
Remind students to study the diagrams in questions 1 and 2 carefully. For question 1 they should decide what proportion each diagram represents, and for question 2, they should notice what's <u>different</u> in each graph, e.g. only A begins above the zero point. They can then discuss the most likely answers for questions 1–4 briefly in pairs.

Questions 5–10
Let them read through the rest of the questions and make sure they know exactly what they have to do for questions 8–10, which is a particularly demanding task. When checking questions 5–7, draw students' attention to items that are mentioned as a distraction but then eliminated, e.g. '… *text messaging … I'll leave that to you. OK, so you won't cover text messaging …*' and warn them to be alert for this in the exam.

IELTS Vocabulary Builder *(p. 91)*

The exercises in this section can either be completed for homework or in class time.

Unit 8 Key

Lead-in *(p. 82)*
1 A (Emergency) Exit
  B Hotel
  C Thunderstorm
  D Biological hazard
  E No motor vehicles
  F Ticket office
  G Stop
  H Fire alarm
  I Drinking Fountain
  J CCTV camera
2 *Example answers*
  Traffic lights (red for stop, green for go); double yellow lines on road (No Parking); red cross or red crescent for emergency medical assistance; skull and crossbones on a bottle (poison); XXX on a letter (kisses); 'smiley' symbols in text messages and emails; thumbs up sign in some cultures (Good/ OK); raised thumb in some cultures (to ask for a lift); gestures for 'come here', 'go away', 'stop', etc;

3 *Example answers*
  Advantages:
  • may be quicker to read and understand than verbal descriptions (eg when driving)
  • can be understood by speakers of any language
  • have more impact than words
  Problems:
  • may not be easy to understand
  • can only give limited information
  • may be different in different countries

Focus on grammar *(p. 83)*
1 1 Informal 2 Formal 3 Permission
   4 Obligation 5 Prohibition
2 1 You can't ~~to~~ park here.
   2 … we <u>had to</u> pay …
   3 He <u>couldn't</u> …
   4 … students <u>will be allowed to</u> use …
3 1 the infinitive
   2 was/wasn't allowed to; will/won't be allowed to, will/won't be permitted to
   3 had to; will have to

5 *Suggested answers*
  1 will have to
  2 are allowed/permitted
  3 is prohibited/forbidden/not permitted
  4 had to
  5 will not be allowed to

Focus on listening 1 *(p. 84)*

1 A 2 C 3 B 4 short 5 your body
6 less powerful 7 high 8 internal
9 weak 10 tested

Focus on writing 1 *(p. 86)*

1 1 Five
  2 They represent two periods of time: 1998–99 and 2001–02
  3 The percentage of households in the UK owning the equipment.
  4 Telephone
  5 Internet connection
2 1 Telephone.
  2 Internet connection – its popularity increased by more than four hundred per cent; Mobile telephone – it became more than twice as popular.
  3 Telephone – its popularity fell by one per cent.
3 1 True
  2 False (almost/just under half/50%)
  3 False (Just over/slightly more than a third)
  4 True
  5 True
  6 False (There are more Russian than Dutch speakers. The percentage of Malay and Dutch speakers is exactly the same.)
  7 False (There are more than twice as many)
  8 False (Polish)
5 2 *Example answers*
  a the percentage of PCs …
  b the level of expenditure/how much money people spent
  c the number of people in prison/the level of imprisonment
  d during the period 2000 to 2005

6 1 31%
  2 Highest: US, Sweden; Lowest: Greece
  3 *(Example answers)* The US has (exactly) twice as many PCs per hundred people as the EU average. / The percentage of PCs in the US is (exactly) double that in the EU as a whole.
Example answer
The bar chart shows the number of PCs per hundred people in the EU as a whole and also in nine countries in 2001. The country with the highest number of PCs, the USA, had 62 per hundred people, which was exactly twice as many as the EU average. The country with the next highest figure was Sweden with 56. The two countries with the lowest percentage of PCs were Spain (17) and Greece (9) respectively.

Focus on speaking 2 *(p. 88)*

1a See Student's book, p. 168.

Focus on writing 2 *(p. 89)*

1 1 Analyse 2 Plan 3 Write 4 Check
3 1 Introduction 2 Arguments for
  3 Arguments against 4 Conclusion

Focus on listening 2 *(p. 90)*

1 B 2 C 3 C 4 A 5–7 (in any order) A, D, E
8 B 9 A 10 C

IELTS Vocabulary Builder *(p. 91)*

Across
2 standby 5 search engine 7 spam
9 hacker 10 surf 11 log
12 space (NB *cyberspace* is one word)
Down
1 file 3 download 4 line 5 scroll 6 chat room
8 website

9 ▶ Earth matters

To set the ball rolling ...

Present the advertisement below, as a handout or an overhead transparency, and give students time to talk about it in pairs. Don't explain that it's a spoof – hopefully they will discover this themselves. Then open a class discussion and use this to gauge their awareness of environmental issues and their attitudes to them.

Want the real facts on climate change?
Read on...

FACT Environmentalists only worry about things that will happen in the future – but many of us won't be around then.

FACT Nobody wants to hear about climate change. It's depressing and doesn't even affect us.

FACT Lots of people want cheap holidays by air, so what's the problem?

Note: This was part of a 'spoof' advertisement by an environmental organisation called SPURT, which opposes unlimited expansion of the aviation industry (see their entertaining website at www.unlimited-spurt.org).

If you have time, focus on the environmental problems of air travel for a few moments: e.g. the growth in cheap air fares and budget airlines (encouraging more air travel), the expansion of many airports (destroying the countryside and residential areas), noise and air pollution, the possibility of a 'green tax' on aviation, etc. This is an additional topic to those in the unit, and will yield some useful vocabulary.

Lead-in *(p. 94)*

Give students a few moments to identify the three environmental topics and then give them time to discuss questions 2 and 3 in pairs. Use the feedback phase to elicit/teach as much topic vocabulary as possible and also take the opportunity to check pronunciation as necessary.

Focus on speaking 1 *How green are you? (p. 94)*

1 Introduce the important expressions in the Essential language box. You could give brief practice by asking topical questions like: *What's the temperature today, do you think? What film is on at the cinema at the moment?* or general knowledge ones like: *What's the fastest*

animal/deepest ocean? etc. Before students begin to discuss the quiz, check understanding of the term 'green' in the heading and also of useful topic expressions in the quiz, including: *environmentally friendly, renewable resource, hazardous waste,* and *junk mail.* Discuss results briefly before students check answers.

2 Introduce the Essential language first and make sure students understand when these phrases are used. Practise briefly, paying particular attention to appropriate stress and intonation. You may need to clarify *get about* (travel to different places) in the first question. Afterwards, ask students to say which is the most and least green option in questions 1 and 2, and why. You could finish by asking them to say how green they think they are (e.g. marks out of ten) on the basis of their answers in this section.

3 These points are suitable for pair discussion or for more formal exam practice. In either case, give students the opportunity to think about the two questions for a few moments and also to ask about vocabulary they need to describe environmental issues in their country.

Focus on reading 1 *Stop the smog! (p. 96)*

1 This is best done with books closed. Write the sub-headings on the board and invite speculation about what each section will contain, without confirming or rejecting any of the suggestions. Remind students how important it is to study headings and sub-headings (See Exam Link p. 52).

2 Point out that taking a moment to predict the kind of vocabulary you're likely to find in a text also helps you read (and listen) more effectively.

3 Ask students to look through the questions and guess answers (without confirming or rejecting any). Set a time limit for the task to discourage over-careful reading. After checking, ask which reading skill they used to locate each part of the text (mainly scanning).

Exam Practice
Read through the introduction, then ask students to underline key words in questions 1–4. Draw their attention to the Tip boxes in the margin and point out that deciding where to find relevant information in a text is an important exam skill which saves unnecessary reading and time. Check that students understand the instructions before they begin each task.

Monitor and guide weaker students in the right direction, if necessary. Let them compare answers and, when checking, ask students to give reasons for their answers.

When checking questions 8–12, it's worth clarifying the difference between F and NG answers. If you make a False statement negative, it becomes true according to information in the text (e.g. Q 10 Cars <u>don't</u> produce the majority of greenhouse gases; Q12 <u>Not fewer</u> but <u>more</u> children are admitted to hospital); This does not work with **Not Given** statements because the information they contain is not mentioned in the text.

Focus on grammar 1 *Cause and effect (p. 98)*

Make sure everyone has underlined the correct expressions in exercise 1. Explain/clarify the expressions as necessary (e.g. *trigger*).

2/3 Discuss the questions in exercise 2 as a class. Check that everyone has filled in the box in exercise 3 a) correctly before they begin exercise 3 b).

Focus on speaking 2 *Expressing degrees of agreement (p. 99)*

Focus on the Essential language first, and practise by putting a range of fairly contentious opinions to students, or put these on paper and let students practise in pairs. Make sure they can use the phrases confidently, and with appropriate stress and intonation. Monitor the pairwork and encourage students to give examples from their personal experience if possible. Ask pairs to report back briefly on their discussions afterwards and use the feedback phase to input useful language.

Focus on reading 2 *How children saved the river (p. 100)*

As an introduction, and also to encourage prediction, write the text title on the board and circle the word 'save'. Ask for ideas about why a river might need to be saved. If 'pollution' is suggested, encourage students to give some specific examples of how a river can become polluted. You could also take it a step further and ask what kind of things they think children could do to save a river in the circumstances they've mentioned.

1 Limit the time for this task to underline the importance of skimming skills in forming a general picture of a text before answering exam questions. At this stage you could also draw students' attention to the three words which are glossed below the text at this stage.

2 Read through the Exam Link and point out that there is more than one kind of multiple choice question. Ask what the difference is between questions 9 – 11 (more than one correct answer) and question 12 (one correct answer). You could also rehearse a basic **Task approach** for all these tasks:
- Study the question underlining key words if possible
- Find the relevant part of the text quickly (Reading skill?)
- Study that section very carefully (Reading skill?)
- Look for *parallel expressions* in the text which match key words in the question.

Point out two very common kinds of wrong answers:
- Statements which include <u>words from the text</u> but give different information
- Statements which contain information that <u>sounds</u> true but which isn't mentioned in the text.

Make sure students notice the two TIP boxes in the margin. Ask them to complete the first before they begin questions 1–3 and check this. Point out that there is a Tip box for each of the three remaining tasks and that they should complete each one.

To give students a more realistic exam experience, let them work through all four exam tasks before comparing answers and checking. Monitor while they work to give in-task feedback and encouragement, and to help steer them in the right direction if necessary. When checking, ask students to justify their answers.

Focus on grammar 2 *–ing v infinitive (p. 102)*

Read through the Exam Link and the introduction. Point out that an easy way to check whether a verb is followed by an -*ing* form or an infinitive (or both) is to look in a good dictionary such as the Longman Exams Dictionary. Remind students that when they make a note of a new verb, they should include an example which shows how it is used in context.

IELTS Vocabulary Builder (p. 103)

The exercises in this section can either be completed for homework or in class time.

Unit 9 Key

Lead-in (p. 94)

1 *Suggested answers*
  A air pollution/exhaust fumes
  B waste disposal
  C flooding/climate change/global warming

Focus on speaking 1 (p. 94)

1 D
2 B The cooker uses approximately 10 per cent more power than a freezer and 400 per cent more power than the washing machine or TV.
3 C **4** B **5** C **6** C **7** A **8** A **9** C **10** A

Focus on reading 1 (p. 96)

1 *Suggested answers*
  • Information about the gases such as oxygen or nitrogen that make up the air, and also about substances which contribute to air pollution, such as exhaust fumes.
  • Information about sources of pollution, such as cars and lorries, factories, etc.
  • Information about the health problems caused by breathing polluted air.

2 *Suggested answers*
  1 *upper atmosphere, gases, ozone*
  2 *motor vehicles, traffic fumes, industrial processes*
  3 *asthma attack, lungs, doctors*

3 *Example answers*
  1 It contaminates rivers, streams and lakes, damages buildings and is a danger to wildlife. It also makes breathing problems worse.
  2 Ozone forms a layer in the upper atmosphere which helps to protect the earth from the sun's rays. However, it has a bad effect on people with breathing problems at ground level.
  3 Motor vehicles, industry and waste disposal (burning rubbish)
  4 Bronchitis, cancer, asthma
  5 1.5 billion

1 1 H 2 B 3 I 4 D 5 acid rain 6 dioxins
  7 motor vehicles/traffic fumes
  8 T *... reducing resistance to infection*
  9 T *Doctors advise sufferers to ... avoid exercise*
  10 F They only produce 15% of worldwide greenhouse gases.
  11 NG
  12 F *The number ... has more than doubled...*

Focus on grammar 1 (p. 98)

1 1 contributes to 2 cause 3 are (largely) responsible for ... 4 lead to 5 trigger
2 1 contributes to 2 trigger 3 lead to

3b 1 are responsible for/cause
  2 contribute to 3 causes
  4 caused by/as a result of
  5 led to

Focus on reading 2 (p. 100)

1 *Suggested answers*
  1 The Funan River; in Chengdu City in China
  2 Pupils at the Longjianglu Primary School in Chengdu
  3 It had become extremely polluted.

2 *Questions 1–3*
  C *they sent a letter to the (then) mayor (line 13)*
  E *a one-day field study (12)*
  F They *appealed to all city residents to ... water (18)*
  Tip: sections B, C
  (answers in any order)
  Questions 4–6
  Tip: section D
  4 T *a correspondent (line 27)*
  5 F *His son became ill (29–31)*
  6 F *The doctor blamed the polluted water .. (31–32)*
  7 NG
  8 T *a two-week investigation (33–34)*
  Questions 9–11
  Tip: sections E, F
  (answers in any order)
  9 A *Shanty towns ... were all bulldozed to make way for ... (lines 45–47)*
  10 C *a 16-kilometre river course was dredged ... (43–45)*
  11 F *A Flowing Water Garden was set up ... (51–52)*
  Question 12
  Tip: section G
  12 C *(63–66)*

Focus on grammar 2 (p. 102)

1 washing **2** to treat; discharging **3** visiting
4 to get **5** to raise; selling **6** writing; to take
7 to give up; smoking **8** to do; spending

IELTS Vocabulary Builder (p.103)

1 1 f) 2 h) 3 c) 4 g) 5 j) 6 i) 7 a)
  8 d) 9 e) 10 b)
3 1 atmospheric 2 beneficial 3 commercial
  4 comparative 5 cultural 6 democratic
  7 economic/ical 8 effective 9 resistant
  10 scientific 11 suburban 12 technological
4 1 tools 2 diseases/illnesses 3 (motor) vehicles
  4 (domestic) appliances 5 (the) media
  6 educational institutions 7 reference books
  8 (civic) amenities 9 aircraft 10 materials

10 ▶ Health check

To set the ball rolling ...

Practise topic vocabulary with the following pair activity.* Prepare two different lists, A and B, set out like the one below. You can vary the vocabulary to suit your students' level and needs but try to include more than one part of speech.

Explain the rules. They must take it in turns to explain each word on their list until their partner guesses it. They shouldn't mention the word itself or make the explanation too easy. When their partner has recognised the word, s/he should write it in the space provided on their own sheet. At the end pairs compare lists and check spelling.

Suggest they start by identifying the part of speech, and begin with an example, e.g. temperature: *This is a noun. It's how hot or cold your body is. If you're ill you often measure this using a special instrument. You can say: 'He's got a high ...'*, etc.

Give students a chance to ask (privately) about any words they don't know before they begin. Monitor carefully and check meanings thoroughly afterwards.

A Your words	Your partner's words
1 diet	....
2 to examine	....
3 surgeon	....
4 vitamin	....
5 healthy	....
6 muscle	....

Other possible words: *clinic, drug, joint, medicine, operation, nerve, nurse, pill, to treat, X-ray.*

* based on an idea in *Working with Words*, CUP, 1986, by Ruth Gairns and Stuart Redman

Lead-in (p. 104)

1 Introduce the task and check vocabulary if necessary e.g. *brain, joint, shade, distinguish.* It's also useful to revise key expressions for speculation (See Essential language p. 94). Ask students to work in pairs and allow a few minutes for them to discuss ideas. When checking, invite them to suggest the answers they're sure about first, working back to the most speculative. If you have time, you could usefully extend the discussion by asking students to enlarge on some answers by naming some joints, saying what the four blood groups are, etc.

2 Remind students about the language for admitting a failure first (See Essential language p. 95), and practise as necessary. You may need to talk about yourself and/or feed in a few ideas (eating, exercise, smoking, etc.) to start the pairwork off. Have a brief discussion afterwards, focusing on any useful language that comes up, e.g. *I do regular exercise/push-ups etc. I'm trying to give up smoking. (I'm afraid) I can't resist chocolate/sweets.*

Focus on grammar 1 (p. 105)

This task can be used for diagnostic purposes or for revision. If your students are less confident with basic grammar, it may be helpful for them to work through the section on Countability in the Key language bank (p. 144) before they start.

Focus on speaking 1 *Facts about smoking (p. 105)*

1 Before you start, ask how many smokers there are in the class and elicit *chain smoker, non-smoker* and *ex-smoker.* Check potential problem vocabulary in the questions such as *quit* (4), *addiction* (6) and *crops* (10). It's also worth making sure that students fully understand questions 3 and 10 and reminding them again about the language of speculation (p. 94). It's best if students work with one book between two when they discuss the quiz questions. Discuss their ideas briefly before they check their answers.

2 If there are no ex-smokers in the class, you may have to help with ideas for giving up smoking (e.g. nicotine replacement therapy such as gum or patches, hypnosis, acupuncture, willpower, etc.). Give students time to talk about the other topics and have a brief class discussion afterwards, eliciting useful vocabulary (e.g. *passive smoking*). Point out that this vocabulary will be very relevant to a Task 2 writing task on the topic of smoking later in the unit.

Focus on listening 1 *Countdown to a healthier life (p. 106)*

Let students read through the instructions and task, then ask them to cover the page. Ask what the topic is and how many words they can write for each answer, before drawing their attention to Exam Link at the foot of the page.

Work through some of the questions as a class, asking what <u>kind</u> of answers are required, e.g. time periods (minutes, hours, or months?) in questions 1 and 9; senses (which ones?) in question 5. Give students a few moments to discuss possible answers in pairs and remind them how making these kinds of predictions can make the listening task easier (see Exam Link p. 43).

Focus on writing 1 *Task 2: Presenting the solution to a problem (p. 107)*

Let students work through exercises 1– 3 in pairs, then discuss 4 and 5 as a class.

4 Concentrate first on style and register, asking students to underline inappropriately informal expressions and suggest improvements. Then elicit a range of linking words and expressions (they could refer back to exercise 3 on p. 24 for some examples) and write these on the board. Discuss ideas and then monitor the writing phase carefully to ensure that students have correct models to refer back to.

5 Focus on the Essential language and practise as necessary so that students can use the phrases appropriately and confidently. With less able students it may be necessary to rehearse answers orally first. Monitor the writing phase carefully.

6/7 Let students work in pairs to underline key words in the exam task and decide which questions to circle in the quiz. Afterwards, discuss their choices and reasons briefly.

8/9 Ask students to transfer the headings on to a piece of paper, so they have plenty of room to make notes. Start the ball rolling by eliciting some ideas for the first section and writing them on the board, as a clear model for students to follow. The writing task can be done in class for timed exam practice (allowing 30–35 minutes for writing/checking) or if you feel close monitoring is needed. Otherwise, set as homework.

Note that there is a model answer for this task in the **Writing practice bank** (p. 163), with questions focusing on the criteria for assessment used by examiners.

Focus on listening 2 *Milestones of medicine (p. 109)*

This is not a particularly difficult task but students need to be absolutely clear about what they have to do for each task, so it's worth spending a little time helping them prepare. Clarify 'milestone' if necessary (an important stage in the development of something).

Once students have looked through the questions, get them to cover the page and ask:
- who they are going to hear (Sarah, a student)
- how many main sections there are (three)
- which task needs most careful attention (questions 2–6, the timeline)

Ask them to look at questions 2–6 more carefully. Introduce the term 'timeline' if necessary and check that they understand it. Ask a few check questions:
- How many centuries does the timeline cover? (three)
- What is the earliest date on the timeline? (1615)
- What is the latest date on the timeline? (1895)
- How many medical discoveries are on the timeline? (five)

Finally, go through the two preparation questions in exercise 1 as a class. Check particularly what kind of answer is required in each question.

Focus on speaking 2 *Discussing medical developments (p. 110)*

Focus on the Essential language first, and provide a few more examples to help students understand the communicative role of these expressions. Give models to illustrate appropriate stress and intonation and practise orally so that students can use the expressions confidently.

Ask them to discuss each development in detail before deciding which is the most important, and to try and reach agreement on their answer. Monitor the pairwork and ask pairs to report back on their decisions and reasons.

DIY Learning strategy *Spot the mistake (p. 110)*

Begin with a whole class discussion exploring students' attitudes to mistakes. Ask:
- *Are language mistakes a good thing or a bad thing? Why?* The answer must begin: 'It depends when …' Mistakes in communication can cause problems, sometimes serious ones, e.g. a misunderstanding between a pilot and air traffic controller. Mistakes made while learning can be a good thing if you learn from them.

- *Do you like to be corrected when you make a mistake (or not)?* Again, 'It depends when …'. Students may be happy to be corrected when they're practising new language but not when they're taking part in an interesting discussion.
- *Is it important for the teacher to correct every mistake?* Some students may expect this, so it's worth encouraging them to think how much time this would take and how much it would interrupt activities.
- *Do you know what your most common mistakes are (in speaking/writing)?* If not, why not? Point out that realistic self-assessment is essential to progress.
- *What do you do with corrections on your written work?* Take a straw poll – you'll probably be very depressed! The chances are your students read the final comment and pay little or no attention to your detailed comments.
- *What <u>should</u> you do with corrections on your written work?* Elicit ideas and encourage students to put some or all into practice!

Let students identify and correct the mistakes and read through the guidelines. NB It would be helpful if you used the same correction symbols when marking students' written work.

For the **DIY Learning project,** allow class time for students to identify a 'favourite' mistake, with your help if necessary, and be prepared to recommend ways of revising/practising this area of language (e.g. check the Key language bank). Make a note of each student's choice so you can follow up on this and give (hopefully positive) feedback in their next piece of written work.

Focus on grammar 2 *Comparing and contrasting (p. 111)*

1 Check that students can name the animals. When checking, elicit relevant vocabulary such as snake *bite,* bee or wasp *sting,* snake *venom,* to be *allergic to …* (e.g. one person in every 200 is *allergic to* bee and wasp venom). Make sure everyone has written the figures next to the animals as this information is needed later.

2 Either let students answer these questions individually or deal with them as a class. Clarify expressions as necessary when checking.

3 Keep as oral practice unless you feel your students would benefit from making a written record of their sentences.

Focus on writing 2 *Task 1: Describing data (p. 112)*

As this task uses language from the previous section, it's best if it can follow on immediately. If this is not possible, begin by reminding students about the relevant expressions.

Note that there is additional Task 1 practice on a health topic in the **Writing practice bank** (p. 164) with questions focusing on interpreting data, and also a gapped model answer.

IELTS Vocabulary Builder *(p. 113)*

The exercises in this section can either be completed for homework or in class time.

Unit 10 Key

Lead-in *(p. 104)*
See Student's book, p. 168.

Focus on grammar 1 *(p. 104)*
1 … aren't <u>any</u>/<u>many</u> sports facilities …
2 … too <u>many</u> toys …
3 ✓
4 Both <s>of</s> Apple and IBM …
5 … <u>a</u> few minutes.
6 … <u>any</u> children.
7 … all <s>the</s> kinds of music.

8 ✓
9 … <u>a lot of</u>/<u>a great deal</u> of money …
10 Every hotel room … <u>is</u> full. (or: <u>All</u> the hotel rooms <u>are</u> …)

Focus on speaking 1 *(p. 105)*
See Student's book, p. 168.

Focus on listening 1 *(p. 106)*
1 20 minutes (mins)   2 hands; feet   3 oxygen level
4 lungs   5 taste; smell   6 breathing
7 exercising   8 10% (ten per cent)   9 5 years
10 has never smoked

Focus on writing 1 (p. 107)

1 *Suggested answer*

Text B is more suitable because it is written in a more formal, less personal style.

2 **1** **A** (e.g. *But there's a problem. That would cost less.*)

2 **B** (*can be … treated, to be manufactured …*)

3 **A** (e.g. *pretty (new), has been around for ages Thank goodness, pricey*)

4 **B** (e.g. *while, However, After all, Another, which*)

3 **1** many **2** relatively **3** have been in existence **4** centuries **5** Fortunately **6** expensive

4 *Example answers*

1 … not surprisingly, older people have difficulty in understanding/using the latest devices/gadgets.

2 … is sold in plastic containers, which is unnecessary and creates an enormous amount of/a huge quantity of/a great deal of waste/rubbish.

3 … who have moved to the city recently in search of employment/a job and accommodation/a place to live, will be disappointed.

5 *Example answers*

1 It is generally accepted that TV is responsible for/is to blame for …

2 Many people argue that it is the government's responsibility to …

3 It appears that global warming is responsible for … ; that the extreme weather we've been experiencing is the result of/is caused by global warming.

9 See model answer in Writing practice bank *p. 163*

Focus on listening 2 (p. 109)

Questions 1–10

1 C   2 Italy   3 1628   4 pressure   5 General
6 Germany   7 A   8 B   9 C   10 B

DIY Learning strategy (p. 110)

1 G (*gives*), A (*about the number*)

2 T (*was*); P (*increase in*)

3 WO (*always have*); Sp (*health*)

Focus on grammar 2 (p. 111)

1 See Students' book *p. 168*.

2 **1** By comparison, By contrast

2 while, whereas

3 By contrast

4 are responsible for/cause *the deaths of …*

3 *Example answers*

Bees cause about 22 deaths each year **whereas** spiders are only responsible for two to four. Crocodiles kill from 600–800 people a year. **By contrast**, snakes are responsible for between 50 and 100 thousand deaths.

Focus on writing 2 (p. 112)

1 **1** 4

2 percentages of total deaths

3 *Example answer*

The diagram shows the percentages of total deaths caused by four main groups of diseases in both the more economically developed and the less economically developed world.

2 **1** diseases of the circulatory system

2 infectious and parasitic diseases

3 infectious and parasitic diseases

3 **a)** **1** almost/nearly/slightly less than

2 By contrast/comparison

3 1.2%

b) **4** while/whereas

5 cause/account for/are responsible for

4 *Example answers*

Cancers **cause** 21% of deaths in the more economically developed world **whereas** they only **account for** 9.5% of deaths in the less economically developed world.

Diseases of the respiratory system **are responsible for** 8.1% of deaths in the more economically developed world. **By contrast**, they only **cause** 4.8% of deaths in the less economically developed world.

IELTS Vocabulary Builder (p. 113)

1 **1** treatment; Casualty **2** injuries **3** cure **4** prescription **5** specialist

2 **1** Neurology **2** Cardiology **3** Physiotherapy **4** Psychiatry

3 **1** up of **2** in **3** on **4** of **5** at **6** between; on **7** by **8** from

4 **1** c **2** d **3** a **4** b

11 ▶ Science of happiness

To set the ball rolling ...

Ask students to define 'happiness'. Give one or two examples, e.g. 'Happiness is being with your family/having lots of money,' and invite comments and alternative suggestions.

Lead-in *(p. 116)*

Let students study the pictures and encourage them to consider the pros and cons for each situation, e.g. success at work may be satisfying and may be rewarded with a good salary, but it may also involve a lot of hard work and stress, which could have a negative effect on your home life, relationships, and health.

Monitor discussions of questions 1 and 2 and use the feedback stage as an opportunity to input any additional relevant language.

Focus on reading 1 *The formula for happiness (p. 117)*

It's worth reminding students that the aim is to get a very general idea of content –there's no need for detail at this stage. Ask them to underline key words in questions 1–5, and to number the main paragraphs 1–5. This makes it easier, especially for lower level students, to refer to relevant sections when checking.

Monitor progress while students complete tasks 1 and 2, and encourage them to compare answers before checking.

Optional additional activities

A Guessing unknown vocabulary

1 Underline the following words in the text and study the context, then:
   • say what **part of speech** they are
   • try to guess their **general meaning**.

   1 quantify (paragraph 1)   4 self-esteem (2)
   2 concluded (2)   5 scenarios (3)
   3 adaptability (2)   6 findings (5)

2 Match each word with one of the dictionary meanings below.

   a) ability to change to suit a new situation
   b) decide that something is true after studying all the information you have
   c) description of a possible situation
   d) feeling that you deserve to be respected and liked
   e) measure (Vb)
   f) results of a study

Answers

1 1 Vb, 2 Vb (past tense), 3 N, 4 N, 5 N (plural), 6 N (plural)

2 1 e), 2 b), 3 a) 4 d), 5 c), 6 f)

B Speaking/Vocabulary: Calculate your happiness

This is a slightly simplified version of the questions the formula in the text was based on. It's a fun activity but as it's potentially rather personal, it's best done individually with just the vocabulary and general premise being discussed as a class. It also may not be suitable for very low level students, as it involves quite challenging vocabulary. Allow around 20 minutes, including checking.

Begin by checking vocabulary, e.g. *outgoing, bounce back, setback, immerse yourself, a sense of purpose*. When students have completed the quiz and checked their score, discuss:
• How accurate do you think the result is?
• Is it possible to measure happiness in this way?

CALCULATING YOUR HAPPINESS

Answer each of the following four questions by giving it a mark on a scale of 1– 10. 1 is 'not at all' and 10 is 'to a large extent'.

Personal characteristics (P)

1 Are you outgoing, flexible and open to change?
2 Do you have a positive outlook, bounce back quickly from setbacks, and feel that you are in control of your life?

Existence (E)

3 Are your basic life needs met, in relation to personal health, finance, safety, freedom of choice, and sense of community?

Higher Order Needs (H)

4 Are you able to call on the support of people close to you, to immerse yourself in what you're doing, to engage in activities that give you a sense of purpose?

How to score: Add the scores for questions 1 and 2 together to find the value P. The score for question 3 is value E and for question 4 is value H. Calculate your score according to the formula:

$$P + (5 \times E) + (3 \times H)$$

If you score 10 for every question, you will have a happiness score of 100. Otherwise, the resulting score is a percentage of perfect happiness.

Focus on grammar 1 *Present tenses with future reference (p. 118)*

The tasks in this section assume that students are familiar with conditional sentences and the terminology used in describing them. If your students are less confident with this area of language, you may need to provide extra support and a more step-by-step approach. You may also prefer lower level students to work through the section on the conditionals in the Key language bank (p. 143) before continuing.

Focus on speaking 1 *Discussing future plans (p. 119)*

1/2 Check vocabulary (including *make a difference* = to have an important effect on something or someone) and instructions beforehand. Let students work individually before comparing results and discussing reasons for their choices. Afterwards it's interesting to compare some of the results as a class, e.g.
  • How many people chose 'Be happy/enjoy life/have fun' first?
  • Which other items were in most people's top 4?
  • Which items were least popular?
  • Were certain items chosen more by men than women (and vice versa), e.g. 'Get a good job/career' or 'Make a difference/help people'?

3 Read through the Essential language as a class and practise as necessary. As the examples show, this language links well with time clauses in Focus on grammar 1, so remind students about this briefly, if need be. Monitor pairwork and give feedback.

Focus on reading 2 *The pursuit of happiness (p. 120)*

Exercises 1 and 2 introduce the topic and help students tune into quite a challenging text. They also provide extra practice in interpreting and describing diagrams.

1 Give students time to study the bar graph, allowing for the fact that there may be quite a lot of interest, especially if a student's own country is included. Ask questions to the whole class and guide the discussion of question 3 if necessary (see notes in Key).

2 If you have time you could insert a brief writing practice here. Ask students to imagine this is a Task 1 topic in the Writing paper and write a suitable introductory sentence.

3 Ask students to work individually and then compare answers. When checking, ask them to mention words or phrases that helped them choose the answers.

Questions 1–5
It's worth reminding students about the difference between this and the similar Locating information task (see Exam Link p. 78). Read through the introduction and Task Approach as a class. It's worth checking <u>why</u> it's best to study the questions first (so you have something specific to look for when you read, and don't waste time trying to understand information that's not important).

Give students time to underline key words in the headings and make sure when checking answers that students can point to expressions that match.

Questions 6–11
Remind students that these questions are always in the same order as information in the text, and also check that they remember the difference between False and Not Given if necessary. (See p. 41 of this book, Focus on reading 1.)

Question 12
Warn students that they <u>must</u> go back to the text rather than rely on memory for this question (See Exam Link p. 96). The information comes from quite a short section but they will need to read very carefully in order to choose the right answer.

4 Remind students that recognising reference links is a key reading skill (see Exam Link p. 13). You could give additional practice by asking students to spot reference links in another text (e.g. section B p. 121).

5 Read through the Exam Link as a class before students work through the questions. If you have time, follow up with some written practice. Give students a suitable written topic (e.g. the problem of debt) and ask them to write sentences using one or more of the linking expressions.

Optional vocabulary practice
This exercise gives further practice in guessing unknown words (see p. 47 in this book, Focus on reading 1) and is best done as a class, especially with lower level students. Begin by establishing the meaning of each base word.

The following adjectives all appear in reading text 2. To work out their meanings:
  • decide **what noun** each word is formed from
  • look at how the word is **used** in the text and in the example

Example: **industrialised** (64) e.g. *Most of the region is heavily industrialised.*
From: *'industry'*. Describes a place with lots of factories, mines, etc.

a) systematic (line 8) e.g. The police carried out a systematic search.
  From '*system*'. Describes an approach which is ...?

b) **individualistic** (40) e.g. *Jones is not a good team player. His style is too individualistic.*
   From …? Describes someone who…?
c) **fatalistic** (44) e.g. *She has a fatalistic attitude towards the exam.*
   From …? Describes someone who …?
d) **consumerist** (79) e.g. *We live in a very consumerist society.*
   From …? Describes a society where …?

You could follow up by asking which adjective(s) students would use to describe:
typical American culture?/their own country or another country they know well?

Answers
a) From *system* (an organised approach or way of working): … well-organised and thorough.
b) From *individual*: … puts themselves rather than other people or society first.
c) From *fate* (the things that happen to you in life, which you cannot change): …believes there is nothing you can do to prevent events from happening.
d) From *consumer* (someone who buys goods or uses services): … buying goods and services is considered very important.

Point out how useful this is as a general strategy for understanding many new words. You may want to give students the following to work on for homework, e.g.

* **occasional** e.g. *I'm very healthy apart from an occasional cold* = happening sometimes but not very often or regularly.
* **unconditional** e.g. *I've received an unconditional offer from Bristol university* = not depending on any condition.
* **invariably** e.g. *It invariably rains during Wimbledon week* = always.
* **formulate** e.g. *The government has formulated a new education policy* = develop/decide all the details of.
* **inconclusive** e.g. *The evidence against him was inconclusive* = not leading to a clear decision or result.

Focus on grammar *Articles (p. 124)*

This exercise provides general revision of the use of articles. Remind students about the points made in the Exam Link on p. 44 and. if you feel they would benefit from a review of the basic rules before they tackle the exercise, refer to the notes on p. 44. Make sure students make use of the Key language bank to check answers rather than rely on you. It would be a good idea to set the practice tasks on pages 141–2 for homework if students haven't completed these already.

Focus on speaking 2 *Answering difficult questions (p. 124)*

1 Introduce the target language by getting students to ask you questions, using prompts such as: Best holiday ever?' and/or 'Historical person/like to meet?'. Point out how useful this language is in giving you time to think, not only in the exam but also in everyday life.

Provide a clear model of the target language and draw students' attention to stress and intonation. Practise using the questions below, in addition to questions 1–4.

* *What's your favourite programme on TV?*
* *If you could have any job in the world, what would you choose?*
* *If you could meet and talk to any famous person (politician/film star/sportsman etc.) and talk to them, who would you choose and why?*

2 Set this up as formal exam practice with one student acting as examiner and one as candidate. Allow about 10 minutes for both interviews and monitor throughout. Afterwards, give exam-focused feedback.

IELTS Vocabulary Builder *(p. 125)*

The exercises in this section can either be completed for homework or in class time.

Unit 11 Key

Focus on reading 1 *(p. 117)*
1 1 Two   2 1,000   3 Higher Order Needs
    4 Psychologist   5 18
2 1 situations/scenarios   2 outlooks   3 weather
    4 with (their) family   5 victories

Focus on grammar 1 *(p. 118)*
1 1 **If clauses**
       If I pass my exams …
       If you haven't arrived by six …
       …if I don't get this job.
    2 **Time clauses**
       When I've finished my studies …
       … before I leave
       … until I get my results

2 1/2/3 when/before/until
   4 present perfect simple
   5 future simple
   6 modal verb
3 *Example answers*
   1 my computer has been mended.
   2 take the exam.
   3 I'll take it again in the autumn.
   4 he comes in.
   5 If I get good marks, ...

Focus on reading 2 *(p. 120)*

1 *Suggested Answers*
   1 Nigeria, Mexico, Venezuela
   2 Italy, Egypt, China
   3 The following distinction is suggested in the original *New Scientist* article :
   Happiness is a mood which is often influenced by events (like being with friends, seeing your favourite team score a goal, hearing music you like, etc.), and can therefore change from moment to moment. **Satisfaction** is how you feel when you step back and judge your life overall. It concerns whether you feel you have the important things you want in life, how much you would change if you could live your life again, etc.

2 *Suggested answers*
   1 It shows (a comparison between) average income and happiness levels over a period of approximately fifty years.
   2 Income increased from approximately $8,000 in 1957 to approximately $22,000 in 2002 / People earned almost three times as much in 2002 as they did in 1957.
   3 Happiness levels remained fairly steady at about 30%.
   4 Higher income levels do not make people happier. As people's incomes increase, their expectations and desires also rise, so it becomes harder for them to feel satisfied with what they have.

3 1 B   2 A   3 C
   Exam Practice (p.121–123)
   Questions 1–5
   1 Section D   ii
   2 Section F   iii
   3 Section G   vi
   4 Section H   i
   5 Section I   iv
   Questions 6–11
   6 **T** (31–33 *he has recorded fifteen different academic definitions.*)
   7 **F** (48–49 *you don't have to feel inferior .... your ability*)

8 F (These are described as important sources of satisfaction in Japan. The main sources of satisfaction for Americans include personal success and self-expression)
9 NG
10 F (66–69 *Study after study ... ... hand in hand with average income.*)
11 T (71–74 *young adults who focus on money ...than others*)
Question 12
12 A and E
4 1 Professor Ruut Veenhoven
   2 the word 'happiness'
   3 happiness
   4 People from Japan, China and South Korea
   5 satisfaction
   6 that the average level of happiness is not changing
5 1 a) Furthermore
      b) However, Meanwhile, on the other hand
      c) So
   2 a) However, Furthermore, on the other hand
      b) Meanwhile
      c) on the other hand (after *on the one hand*)

Focus on grammar 2 *(p. 124)*

1 – 2 – 3 the 4 the 5 a 6 – 7 an 8 –
9 – 10 – 11 – 12 the 13 – 14 – 15 –
16 – 17 – 18 the 19 the 20 –

IELTS Vocabulary Builder *(p. 125)*

1 1 **dis**satisfaction 2 **in**equality 3 **un**employment
   4 **in**security 5 **dis**agreement 6 **mis**understand
   7 **un**happy 8 **in**flexible 9 **un**interesting
   10 **mis**interpret 11 **in**appropriate 12 **dis**courage
2 1 adaptability 2 existence 3 health
   4 expectation 5 stability 6 difference
   7 achievement 8 ability 9 co-operation
   10 friendliness 11 observation 12 growth
3 1 self-employed 2 self-discipline
   3 self-expression 4 self-esteem
   5 self-confident 6 self-contained

12 ▶ Buildings and structures

To set the ball rolling ...

Ask students to name the most famous building in the town you're in now, or in another well-known city if that is more appropriate. Use this as an opportunity to remind them about relevant language for the Interview, e.g. expressing an opinion, speculating and answering difficult questions (Essential language pp. 14, 28 and 124).

Lead-in (p. 126)

1 Let students discuss the pictures briefly in pairs before establishing the correct answers. Invite speculation about the oldest and most recent but avoid confirming or denying any answers at this stage.

2 Allow time for students to work individually before comparing answers in pairs. When checking, ask students to say which words or phrases helped them to identify the correct picture, e.g. *varying in height between … (D), a single block of limestone (C)*, etc.

3 Have a brief open class discussion, again emphasising the importance of framing an answer appropriately: e.g. *The structure I'd really like to visit is …*

Focus on grammar *Participle clauses (p. 127)*

Check understanding of the term '**participle**' by asking for examples of past or present verb participles. Establish how each of the two kinds is formed (+-*ed* or irregular; +-*ing*) and ask which tenses each participle is found in (present perfect, and other perfect tenses; present progressive and other progressive tenses).

Read through the Exam Link and introduction to exercise 1, making sure students are completely clear about how the table is organised before continuing. With lower level students, you may want to work through the section as a class, clarifying the points as you go. Otherwise let students work in pairs. For exercise 2, you could ask students to copy the layout of the table in exercise 1, adding one extra row to allow for examples from the three texts.

Focus on speaking 1 *Discussing buildings (p. 128)*

1 Introduce this topic by asking a question likely to elicit a negative answer (e.g. *What do you enjoy most about*

studying grammar?) then talk through the Essential language and example. Practise further by asking questions like: *What do you think of the city museum? Who's your favourite English composer?* etc., paying particular attention to appropriate stress and intonation.

Read through the instructions for the pairwork and make sure students know they have to give <u>true</u> answers, only making negative comments when appropriate. Go through a few suitable questions and monitor students' conversations.

Exam Practice
To give students a more realistic exam experience, let one 'candidate' work through both Parts 1 and 2, before swapping roles with his/her partner. Monitor the interviews and note key points for general feedback at the end. Begin by organising students into pairs with a designated examiner and candidate and rearranging seating as far as possible so students can face each other exam-style.

2 If your students are studying away from home, it's worth mentioning in relation to question 1 that they can talk about <u>either</u> their home town <u>or</u> their adopted town (or even both) as long as they make this clear. For questions 2 and 3, remind them about ways of introducing negative comments if necessary.

3 Check that students remember the procedure for this task, and remind them about mindplans if necessary. Make sure everyone has a pen and paper for note-taking and remind 'examiners' to keep an eye on timing, allowing about 1 minute for preparation and 2 minutes' speaking time, before asking one or two closing questions. As this is the last practice for parts 1 and 2 of the speaking test, give plenty of positive feedback at the end and finish with a round-up of key advice.

Focus on writing 1 *Describing objects (p. 128)*

1 If you have time, you could include the following additional topic vocabulary practice. You will need to draw items A–G on the board or produce handouts.

Additional vocabulary practice

1 Match each expression to the correct drawing A–G.
  1 Angle
  2 Curved line
  3 Diagonal line
  4 Horizontal line
  5 Oval
  6 Parallel lines
  7 Vertical line

2 Answer the following questions by choosing letter(s) from the alphabet which:
  a) consist of just two diagonal lines?
  b) consist of 1 vertical and 1 horizontal line?
  c) consist of just curved lines?
  d) is semi-circular in shape?
  e) have parallel horizontal lines?
  f) are triangular in shape?

  A B C D E F G H I J K L M N O P Q R S T U V W X Y Z

  Answers
  2 a) V, X b) L, T c) C, O, (Q), S d) D e) E, F, Z
    f) A, V

3 Read through the Essential language, and make sure students are completely clear about the difference between **is +** Adj (long/wide etc) and **has a +** Noun (length, width, etc). Practise by asking students to describe a few everyday objects, e.g. the table etc. (*long*); the board/coin/can, etc. (*shape*); the classroom/a pen/a drinks can, etc. *(contain)*; the table/the window/a pair of jeans, etc. *(is made of)*. Let students complete the gapfill exercise and then compare answers.

4 This exercise is suitable for class or homework. With lower level students, practise orally first.

Note that in addition to describing an object in Task 1, students may also be asked to explain how something works. These are less common than questions focusing on presenting data, but they can and do appear from time to time so it is important that students are aware of what's required and have the basic language for the task. There is guided practice for this in the Writing practice bank (p. 165), and it's advisable to go through this as a class. (See the Teaching notes for this in this book, p.58)

Focus on listening 1 *Opera House Tour (p. 130)*

Point out that words like 'duration' and 'departure', which are often found in official forms and notices, are quite formal. The same information is likely to be expressed in a less formal way in the conversation on the tape. For this reason, it's a good idea to think about other ways of expressing these ideas in advance.

Let students work in pairs to discuss questions 2 and 3, and then invite a few guesses without accepting or rejecting any.

Questions 1–10
Read through the Exam Link before playing the recording. Let students compare answers before checking.

Focus on listening 2 *The Itaipu Dam (p. 131)*

First ask students to look at the questions for about 30 seconds, and then cover the page. Ask what the subject is, how many different kinds of question there are, and how many words they have to write for the first section, Point out how important it is to find out as much as possible about the task before listening.

Work through questions 1–3 as a class. For 1, remind students of the point made about words like 'duration' and 'departure' in Focus on Listening 1 and ask them to suggest less formal ways of talking about this information. For 2 and 3, encourage speculation, reminding them how much this helps the listening process. (See Exam Link p. 43)

Questions 1–10
Again ask students to cover the page and check that they know how many answers to choose in the second section and how many words to write for the third. Let students compare answers before checking, and focus on any useful vocabulary, e.g. nouns ending -*ity*: *gravity, capacity, stability*; words meaning 'very large': *massive, immense,* etc.

Focus on speaking 2 *Giving supporting examples (p. 132)*

Read through the Essential language and examples as a class. If possible, prompt a few more questions and give answers of your own, so students hear the expressions as naturally as possible. Practise repeating the target language from the examples, paying special attention to stress and intonation. Write up a few similar questions and give students time to think of supporting examples before eliciting answers.

• Do you think children today eat enough healthy food?
• Do women today have an easier life than their mothers did?

Exam practice

Organise students into pairs with a designated examiner and candidate and rearrange seating as far as possible so students can face each other exam-style. Allow time for them to read through the topics and then monitor the pairwork. As this is the last exam practice, give plenty of positive feedback and end with a round-up of advice for this part of the interview.

Focus on grammar 2 *Unreal conditionals (p. 132)*

The tasks in this section are designed as revision. Unless your students are confident with this area of grammar, you will probably need to provide extra support and a more step-by-step approach. In this case, it may be helpful to begin by revising Type 1 conditionals briefly (see p. 118). Remind students that these describe possible and quite probable events in the future. Check that they can identify the '*if* clause' and '**main clause**,' and that they remember the correct sequence of tenses (see Key language bank, p. 143).

1 When students have studied the example sentences, use 2 and 3 to check the two main concepts (see Key language bank, p. 143).
   Example questions:
   2 Do TV companies spend money on game shows? (Yes); Are they popular? (Yes) – This describes an unreal situation in the present.
   3 Are the teachers on strike now? (No); Is it possible they will go on strike in the future? (Yes); Is it probable? (Not very – compare with *If the teachers go on strike,*) – This describes a future event which is possible but fairly (un)likely.

   When checking, make sure students are clear about the correct sequence of tenses in Type 2 conditionals (see Key language bank, p. 143).

2 Monitor progress and if you feel more support is needed, you could work through exercise 2 in the Key language bank (p. 144) as a class before completing this section.

3/4 Depending on your students' performance, these exercises can be completed in class or for homework.

Note that Type 3 conditionals are not included in the main grammar sections, as they have more limited value in IELTS terms, especially if time is short. However, there are detailed notes on Type 3 conditionals and a practice exercise in the Key language bank (p. 144).

Focus on writing 2 *Presenting the solution to a problem (p. 133)*

Let students study the exam task and ask them to suggest a few causes and solutions before they work through the exercises. Once they've read through problems 1–5, take the first effect a) as an example and ask them to say which problem it matches. They could then find two more effects which also match the same problem (f and l). When students complete the last two columns (Cause and Solutions), they may find it easier to use a larger piece of paper.

The planning and writing phase could usefully be done as timed exam practice in class.

Note that there is an additional Task 2 topic in the Writing practice bank (p. 167) with questions revising the key stages in preparing a Task 2 answer.

IELTS Vocabulary Builder *(p. 135)*

The exercises in this section can either be completed for homework or in class time.

Unit 12 Key

Lead-in (p. 128)

1a) 1 D 2 E 3 B 4 C 5 A

b) NB Students can check answers when they read the descriptions in the next exercise.
(The oldest is the Great Sphinx, c. 2,500. The most recent is the Statue of Liberty, 1884)

2 1 D 2 C 3 A 4 E 5 B

Focus on grammar 1 (P. 127)

1 1 Two. Verbs.
2 One.
3 The main clause. This vast structure
4 Two: Past (-ed) clause and present (-ing) clause
5 Passive

2 Text 3 Completed in 1884 … (Past); subject: it
Text 4 Constructed between 1632 and 1650 … (Past); subject: the entire structure
Text 5 Standing 55 metres high … (Present); subject: this structure

Focus on writing 1 (p.128)

1 1 E 2 D 3 G 4 H 5 B 6 C 7 F 8 A

2 1 circular 2 cubic 3 cylindrical
4 rectangular 5 semi-circular 6 spherical
7 square 8 triangular

3 1 rectangular 2 consists of 3 made of
4 long 5 wide 6 height 7 contains
8 connected to

Example answers

B The aerosol spray can is **cylindrical** in shape. It **consists of** a metal container, a plunger, a valve and a narrow tube which **is made of** plastic. The can is 13 cm **high** by 5 cm **wide/in diameter** and it **contains** hair lacquer mixed with liquid propellant.

C The light bulb is approximately 10 cm **long**. It **consists of** a glass bulb, which is mainly **spherical** in shape, electrical contacts, which **are connected to** the filament **by** wires, and a support. The bulb **contains** inert gas.

Focus on listening 1 (p.130)

1 Preparation
1 *How long …?* e.g. *How long does it take/last?*
2 *When …?* e.g. *When does it go/leave/start?*
3 *How much …?* e.g. *How much is it?/does it cost?*

2 2 (possibly, e.g. *every 2 hours*) 3, 7, 8, 10

Questions 1–10

1 architecture 2 half hour 3 23 4 full-time
5 private tour 6 technical 7 2 hours/hrs 8 140
9 breakfast 10 9250 7250

Focus on listening 2 (p. 131)

1 *Example answers*
Completion date – When was it finished/built?
Material – What is it made of?

Questions 1–10

1 1982 2 20 billion 3 concrete 4 height
5 capacity 6/7 B, D (in either order) 8 heel
9 toe 10 foundation

Focus on grammar 2 (p. 132)

1 1 If more people travelled by public transport,
2 … unless they were popular.
3 If the teachers went on strike,
4 … if there was an earthquake.

2 1 True (e.g. sentences 2 and 4 in exercise 1)
2 False (only after the conditional clause)
3 True (also *unless* as in sentence 2)
4 False (also modal verbs like *might* and *could* as in sentences 3 and 4)

3 *Example answers*
1 If there was more cheap accommodation near the college, more students would live in the area.
2 I wouldn't phone you so late unless I had important news (to tell you).
3 Children wouldn't behave so badly in school if their parents were stricter with them at home.
4 If the government didn't spend so much on the army it might be able to afford to fund more basic services.

4 *Example answers*
1 If children took more exercise, there wouldn't be a growing problem of obesity amongst the young.
2 Drug dealers would go out of business if people didn't buy from them.
3 If we invested more money in preventative medicine, it would reduce the cost of caring for sick people.
4 Many more people could go to university if they didn't have to pay tuition fees.
5 If air travel were more expensive, fewer people would be able to travel abroad.

Focus on writing 2 (p. 133)

2 1 h), k) 2 c), g) 3 d), i) 4 b), e), j)
5 a), f), l)

IELTS Vocabulary Builder (p. 135)

1 1 Steel 2 Brick 3 Stone 4 Timber

2 1 arch 2 column 3 dome 4 tower

3 1 span 2 storey 3 foundation 4 plumbing

4 /e/ frame, great, laid, shape, weight
/ai/ design, height, light, site, type
/iː/ chief, deep, heat, key, metre

▶ Writing practice bank:
Key and Teaching notes

Practice 1 *(p. 156)*

Teaching notes

Let students read the text carefully and ask some general check questions, e.g.

- Does the writer agree /partly agree/disagree with the statement?
- When do we find out the writer's overall opinion?
- How does the writer introduce the topic?

After checking answers, you could also help students to notice some other features of the model answer, e.g.

- How often is the pronoun *I* used?
- How many examples of 'communications' (modern or otherwise) are mentioned?
- What proportion of the essay do the introduction and conclusion make up? (around a third)

Key

2 1 Four
   2 Introduction, explaining the background to the topic; Reasons for agreeing with the opinion in the question; Reasons for disagreeing with the opinion in the question; Conclusion, balancing the argument.
   3 However,
   4 In addition,
   5 On the other hand,
   6 Telephoning, emailing and texting
   7 The fact that letters are more formal and carefully composed than emails
   8 Letters
   9 *Example answer*:
      letter writing <u>was</u> … (line 1, past simple)
      we <u>have developed</u> … (2, present perfect)
      <u>would have written</u> … (4, Type 3 conditional)
      we <u>prefer</u> … (4, present simple)
      we <u>can</u> receive … (7, modal verb, present)
      I <u>would</u> … <u>agree</u> … (14, Type 2 conditional)
   10 *Example answer*:
      Paragraph 1: main, faster, (more) direct, personal, (relatively) rare
      Paragraph 2: true, (perfectly) suitable, immediate, (extremely) useful
      Paragraph 3: formal, (carefully) composed suitable, likely, better, important, complex, official, legal
      Paragraph 4: fewer, important, appropriate

Practice 2 *(p. 157)*

Key

1 1 The average age of women at their first marriage
   2 8
   3 1980–98 (18 years)
   4 It rose/went up/increased (slightly).
   5 **In erratum**: The figures for Russia should read **23, 23, 23**. The answer should therefore be Russia. This will be corrected with the second impression of *Focus on IELTS Foundation*.
   6 Sweden
2 1 The number of marriages and divorces per thousand people
   2 8
   3 1981–94 (13 years)
   4 1 (Denmark)
   5 There were fewer marriages/the number of marriages decreased, etc.
   6 5: (UK, Japan, Finland, France, Italy)
   7 There were more divorces/the number of divorces rose, etc.
   8 The USA and Denmark, where the number of divorces fell, and Germany, where the figure remained the same.
   9 Italy
3 1 (a) general trend
   2 rose, had risen
   3 By comparison
   4 over the period
   5 The (only) exception (to this trend)
   6 As we can see from the information,
4 1 general trend   2 the period   3 1994
   4 9.1 (per thousand)   5 France   6 comparison
   7 exceptions   8 Italy
5 1 decrease   2 fell, had fallen   3 increase
   4 the most, the fewest   5 figure

Practice 3 *(p. 159)*

Key

1 1 size/extent
2 the largest/greatest
3 larger
4 the smallest
5 the shortest
6 the highest
7 most/best/well
8 least/worst/not well
2 1 3; introduction, middle/body/detailed description, conclusion
2 No.
3 The table gives information about …
4 As we can see from the data …
5 On the other hand, By contrast,

Practice 4 *(p. 159)*

Key

1 1 Once (line 22).
2 For (see conclusion).
3 Supporters of zoos (6)
4 Those who oppose zoos (14)
5 Two (education and conservation)
6 Two (cruelty and the fact that zoos are <u>not</u> as educational as people think)
7 In addition (11); A further argument (against) (18)
8 However, (23)
9 This applies particularly to … (15)
10 On balance, (I feel that) …

Practice 5 *(p. 160)*

Key

1 1 Graph C (Nepal)
2 Graph A (Bangladesh)
3 Graph B (Kenya)
2 *Suggested answers*
  A 1 12 °C
  2 lasts
  3 remain fairly constant
  4 between …. and
  B 5 The hottest
  6 average around/reach/reach a peak of/rise to
  7 During
  8 fall/drop to

C 9 a minimum (temperature)
10 a maximum (temperature)
3 *Example answers*
  D The temperatures in Cambodia are high throughout the year. During the hottest months from March to May, they reach (a maximum of) around 35 °C, while during the cooler months from December to February, they drop to (a minimum of) around 22 °C. There is little or no rain during January but rainfall increases gradually during the year until it reaches a peak of about 28 cm in October. It then decreases fairly sharply during November and December.
  D Canada has a wide temperature range with a maximum temperature of around 25 °C in July and a minimum of around 9 °C from December to February. Rainfall remains at a constant level of around 8 cm throughout the year.

Practice 6 *(p. 162)*

Key

2 *Suggested answers*
  a) ✓? (could possibly be included in a general introduction to the topic)
  b) ✓ (negative point)
  c) ✗
  d) ✓ (negative point)
  e) ✗
  f) ✓? (only if related to the Internet)
  g) ✗
  h) ✓ (positive point)
3 *Example answers*
  In favour: The Internet is invaluable as a research tool for homework and study projects; Internet use develops computer skills which are likely to be useful in later life.
  Against: Children may be exposed to unsuitable material; Children could neglect other forms of learning.

Practice 7 *(p. 163)*

Key

1 Because of the health risks to the individual (cancer, heart disease, etc.) and the cost to society in health care.

2 Three: increasing the tax on tobacco; banning cigarette advertising; providing advice and support for people who want to give up smoking

3 *Example answers*
  a figures about the number of adult male smokers worldwide and the age when teenagers take up the habit
  b the fact that the link between smoking and cancer has been known for many years
  c the fact that young people may start smoking as a result of peer pressure (the feeling that you must do the same things as other people in your social group)

4 *Example answers*
  • Introduction: the scale of the problem
  • the harmful effects of smoking (on the individual and on society)
  • reasons people smoke and possible solutions to the problem
  • Conclusion

5 *Example answers*
  • *which, and, yet, also, when, Of course, which, since,*
  • *because, also, apart from, such as*
  • *So, despite, so that, Another, In my view, and, also, who*
  • *In conclusion, However, also.*

6 *Example answers*
  Smoking, take up the (smoking) habit, the tobacco industry, (our) addiction to cigarettes, the link between smoking and cancer, smoking-related diseases, (highly) addictive, (the) tax on tobacco, cigarette advertising; quit (smoking)

7 *In my view* (line 12), *I also feel (that)* (line 14), *I believe* (line 15)

8 *has been known* (line 6), *could be used* (line 8), *should be given* (line 14)

9 *must* (line 6), *could* (lines 8, 13) *can* (lines 11, 15) *should* (lines 14, 15)

10 *So why, despite all the evidence, do people still smoke*? This makes the writing more direct and interesting to the reader, and also adds to the variety of structures.

Practice 8 *(p. 164)*

Key

1 1 Smoking related deaths
  2 1990–2030 (40 years)
  3 (percentages of) male smokers; (percentages of) female smokers
  4 (smokers in) the developing world; (smokers in) the developed world

2 1 A sharp/steep   increase/rise
  2 men
  3 male smokers in the developing world (48%)
  4 female smokers in the developing world (7%)
  5 There are **6% more** male smokers in the developing world **than** in the developed world.
  6 There are **over three times more** female smokers in the developed world **than** in the developing world. NB The following answer is also possible: There are more than three times **as many** female smokers in the developed world **as** in the developing world.

3 1 40
  2 responsible for
  3 1990
  4 rise (steeply/sharply); increase (rapidly/sharply)
  5 until
  6 shows
  7 from
  8 largest/greatest/highest
  9 50
  10 higher/greater/more
  11 figure
  12 contrast/comparison
  13 while/whereas
  14 lower/less

Practice 9 *(p. 165)*

Teaching notes

1 Find out if students know what a water tower is and what it's for. Ask where you usually see water towers – high up or low down – and why. Check that students can 'read' the diagram, and clarify vocabulary as necessary e.g. *treatment plant (plant = factory or place where industrial process takes place), sediment, bacteria, feeders (= pipes)*

Let students work individually and then compare answers. Emphasise that you can describe even fairly complicated-looking processes with simple clear vocabulary.

2 Begin by finding out what students know about windmills and check that they can read the diagram. Clarify vocabulary as necessary e.g. *shaft* (long thin piece of metal in an engine or machine that turns and passes on power or movement to another part of the machine). This is best done as class work with weaker students.

Key

1 1 consists of
2 contains
3 is raised
4 is connected
5 vertical
6 remove
7 sends
8 supply

2 *Example answer*

The tower windmill is specially designed to use wind power to drive machinery for grinding corn into flour. It **consists of** a building which is roughly **cylindrical in shape** and approximately 15 metres **high**, with a pointed cap **at the top**. The whole building **is raised** about a metre above ground. **On one side** of the cap there are four sails which **are made of wood** and **on the opposite side** a **circular** fantail, and the two **are connected by** a **horizontal** shaft. The windmill also **contains** various gears which **are connected to** the grinding equipment on the lower floors by a **vertical** central shaft. As the sails turn, they **produce** power which is **transmitted/sent** to the grinding equipment via the gears and shafts. This enables the machinery to grind the corn into flour.

Practice 10 *(p. 167)*

Key

1b) *Example answers*

1 Architectural heritage includes interesting structures from early prehistoric remains to grand buildings like castles and palaces, and from early industrial structures like bridges and tunnels to important modern buildings.

2 Students' own ideas

3 We can see how people built their houses and public buildings and also understand more about the conditions in which people lived in the past.

4 Part of a region's history, a connection between past and present, examples of old construction techniques

5 This obviously depends on the nature of the building, but possible uses include cultural centres, museums, tourist attractions, etc.

6 The cost of repairs and maintenance can be very high; buildings need to be protected from damage and vandalism

7 Providing housing for homeless people, building schools and universities, medical research, etc.

8 Entrance fees, lottery grants, sponsorship, advertising, etc.

Audio script

Unit 2, Focus on listening 1

Letters and sounds 1 (p.17)

EXERCISE 2
1 B-A-C-K-E-R
2 G-A-D-G-E-T
3 C-H-E-R-V-I-L
4 H-E-N-B-A-N-E

EXERCISE 3
1 T-O-A-D H-A-L-L
2 S-A-N-D-R-I-N-G-H-A-M
3 M-A-N-S-F-I-E-L-D P-A-R-K

Unit 2, Focus on listening 2

Introducing listening skills (p.18)

EXERCISE 1

1 For passengers on Platform 4 awaiting the arrival of the 10.24 to Exeter, we regret to inform you that this train is currently running fifteen, that's one-five, minutes late. The delay is due to signalling problems in the Reading area. We apologise for any inconvenience this may cause.

2 Police are continuing to hunt for prisoners who escaped from Longmead Gaol last night. One man has given himself up and police say they are confident of recapturing the rest in the next couple of days. There has been an earthquake measuring 5.5 on the Richter Scale in Japan …

3 Things are fairly quiet at the moment in the city. But for those of you heading onto the motorway the news is not so good, I'm afraid. We're getting reports of a lorry shedding its load on the southbound carriageway near Junction 8. So be prepared for delays.

4 *(SM = Sally Meakin; I = Interviewer; BT = Bill Turnbull)*
SM Right, well, first of all, thanks for coming in. My name's Sally Meakin and this is my colleague, Bill Turnbull …
I Hello.
BT Hi, how's it going?
SM … And what we'd like to do today is find out a bit about you, discover what makes you tick. OK?
I OK.
SM So let's begin. Now you say on your application form that you enjoy a challenge, and I wonder …

5 OK, now the first thing we have to do is to make sure you all know how to get on correctly. So watch me first. You face the back of the horse, take the reins in your left hand like this, right? Put your left foot in the stirrup, grasp the back of the saddle with your right hand like this, and up you go!

EXERCISE 2

1 Short city breaks are very popular these days. And there are some great package deals available this autumn. For example, you can have three nights for the price of two in Paris, staying in a three-star hotel, but only if you're free to travel this weekend …

2 *(TA = Travel agent; C = customer)*
TA Flight Savers, Can I help you?
C Hello, yes, I'm looking for a cheap flight to Sydney.
TA Single or return?

3 A I'm doing a project on Japan as a tourist destination.
B Sounds interesting. Do you get to go there?
A I wish!

4 Hi, Andy. Could you do me a favour? I'm up to my eyes at the moment. Yes. But we need to get those samples to our agent in Washington. Could you give the couriers a ring and arrange a pick-up ASAP? You will? Many thanks.

5 OK everyone! Now on Saturday, there's a trip to see an exhibition of photographs by Julia Margaret Cameron, if you're interested. Cameron was born in 1815, in India, if I remember rightly, and she was one of the first women to become a professional photographer. Anyway, it's a fantastic exhibition …

EXERCISE 3

1 We'll start off in the south east. Here there's quite a bit of cloud around and I think we'll see some bands of rain during the afternoon. As a result, temperatures are unlikely to rise above 15 degrees. Next I'll take the whole of the north and west …

2 Now here's something that might interest you. It's a studio apartment, so OK it's tiny, but it's right in the central business district. And that's 800 dollars a month. It's a pretty good price for the location – what do you think?

3 And now for the financial news. According to a report published in *Home Buyer* magazine, property prices in certain areas have risen 12 per cent in the last year. This means that it's becoming even harder for young people to get a foot on the property ladder.

4 A major power failure left almost all of Italy without electricity yesterday. The blackout extended from the Alps in the north to Sicily in the south, cutting power supplies to around 57 million people. Transport was disrupted as traffic lights broke down and trains and trams stopped running.

5 In my lecture today, I want to look at the work of the Irish writer, Frank O'Connor, who is best known for his short stories. O'Connor was born in Cork, Ireland in 1903. He was an only child and most of his childhood was spent in considerable poverty …

Unit 4, Focus on listening 1

Letters and sounds 2 (p.42)

EXERCISE 1
1 child
2 height
3 great
4 weight
5 flight
6 eye
7 quite
8 break
9 buyer
10 neighbour

EXERCISE 2

1	said, paid	The answer is *said*.
2	many, lazy	The answer is *many*.
3	reason, measure	The answer is *measure*.
4	chief, friend	The answer is *friend*.
5	guess, queue	The answer is *guess*.
6	leisure, seize	The answer is *leisure*.
7	breathe, breath	The answer is *breath*.
8	pretty, plenty.	The answer is *plenty*.

EXERCISE 3

1 Albany A-L-B-A-N-Y
2 Carlisle C-A-R-L-I-S-L-E
3 Mainstay M-A-I-N-S-T-A-Y
4 Channing C-H-A-N-N-I-N-G

Unit 4, Focus on listening 2

International Friendship Club (p.42)

S = Simon; M = Maria

S 2466. Simon speaking.

M Hello. Is that the right number for the International Friendship Club?

S Yes, that's right. How can I help?

M I picked up a copy of your newsletter in the Students' Union, and I was wondering if you could tell me a bit more about the club?

S Yes, of course. We set up the club three years ago as a way of promoting international understanding. So we've been established for a while now. And, there are meetings every Thursday evening, during term time that is.

M Thursday, right.

S Yes, we usually show a film or maybe run a competition of some kind. But mostly it's an opportunity for people to get together, relax, make friends. And we also produce a regular newsletter – I think you said you'd seen a copy of that … ?

M The newsletter? Yes, it looked interesting.

S So you know it's got loads of information about what's on in the area and about living in Britain in general. We also have quite a busy social programme with outings to places of interest like London or Oxford.

M Sounds great.

S And one other thing to mention. We like to encourage people to attend regularly and play a real part in the club. So we give special certificates as a reward for active participation. It's something you can put on your CV, for example.

M I see. And, I meant to ask does it cost anything to join? Is there a fee?

S Yes, membership costs £5 for a term but you can save a bit of money if you pay for the whole academic year. Then it's only £12, instead of £15. That doesn't include special trips. But they're subsidised by the university, so they're not too expensive. The Oxford trip only costs £10, for example.

M So, how do I go about joining?

S Right, well I'll take a few details now if I may, so I can send you a welcome pack. That's got all the information you need. Then if you're happy to go ahead, perhaps you could send us a cheque for your membership fee?

M Fine.

S OK. So could I have your name please?

M Maria Lanzerac.

S Sorry, could you spell that for me?

M Yes, Lanzerac, L-A-N-Z-E-R-A-C.

S Right. And where are you from, Maria? I should be able to tell from your accent but …

M Don't worry. Most people think I'm from Australia but I'm actually South African.

S That's somewhere I've always wanted to go! Now your address. Do you live in the city?

M Yes, I'm staying at 47 March Street, Southville.

S 47 … Sorry, what was the street name again?'

M March Street. Like the month.

S OK. So you haven't got far to come, have you? And how old are you, if you don't mind my asking?

M I'm 22. 23 next month, actually.

S Right. And last but not least, I just need to know what course you're doing?

M Art History. I'm on the MA course.

S Fantastic. Well, I think that's all I need for now. You should get the pack in the post tomorrow. Just give me a call if you've got any questions.

M Thanks. Bye.

Unit 6, Focus on listening 1

Wildlife Film Festival (p.63)

EXERCISE 1

1	2.365%	4	577204
2	1,100	5	01628 351940
3	5.45		

Unit 6, Focus on listening 1

Exam Practice (p.63)

Right, well we come to the part of the programme where we look at what's on in our area. And this week we've got something really rather special to look forward to. It's a Festival of Wildlife Films at the Regent Arts Centre. The festival runs for Saturday and Sunday and it's got something for everyone, whether you're 8 or 80! I've only got time to tell you about a few of the films on offer, but at least it'll give you a flavour of the programme.

OK. So first off on Saturday morning is a film called *My Life as an Ant* which starts at 10.30 a.m, have I got that right? … Yes, 10.30. This is definitely one for the children. The leading character is a tiny ant, just one centimetre long. And he introduces us to his world as he travels around, looking for food to take back to his family. *My Life as an Ant* was made using the latest digital technology, and it comes from Japan. From what I've heard, the close-up images of the insect world are pretty amazing,

OK, well if you're not into creepy-crawlies, and I know some people aren't, we can move from one of the smallest creatures to one of the largest, because there's another great film on Saturday evening. This one's called *Ocean Oasis*. It's an American production and it was filmed in the oceans around the coast of Mexico. It's a film that takes you into the fantastic life and colours of the coral reefs. And there's also some amazing film of scientists swimming side by side with huge sea creatures like giant manta rays and even whales. This is a real adventure for the mind and senses.

Moving on to Sunday, we've got two more great offerings. First at 11 in the morning there's a film from China called *The Mystery of Yunnan Snub-nosed Monkey*. This is very special. It took ten years to make and it's the first real in-depth study of these monkeys which live deep in the forests of south west China. Apparently there's under fifteen hundred of them left now, so they're obviously in real danger of extinction. Anyway it's a wonderful film and it won a TVE Award last year. Not sure what that stands for, exactly … Anybody know? No, no one in the studio knows. I expect one of our listeners will have the answer.

The last film I'm going to tell you about is on Sunday afternoon. It's called *Riverhorse* and it was made by a team of film-makers from the UK. It's the story of a family of hippos living by an African river, and the film follows the family over a two-year period. In that time the film-makers managed to get incredibly close to the hippos as well as to crocodiles and other river animals. *Riverhorse* also won a film award last year – it won the 'Animal Behaviour' category of the Panda film awards.

So that's just four of the fabulous films on offer at the festival but there's plenty more to choose from, as well as competitions and activities for children. For more details, just give the Box Office a ring. The telephone number, if I can just find it … Yes, the number to ring is 973 4617. I'll repeat that 973 4617.

On now to the sporting fixtures for the weekend, and here's Amy to give us the details …

Unit 6, Focus on listening 2

The right to roam (p.65)

T = Tutor; L = Lisa; J = Jamie

T Is everyone here now? Lisa? Jamie? Maria? Good. Well, we're continuing the module on 'Animal Rights' and I think Lisa, you're going to talk to us about your assignment, right?

L Yes.

T And what topic have you chosen?

L The problems of keeping large animals in zoos.

T Fine. And where did you get your information?

L Partly from an article I read, about some research they've done, and also from the Web.

T OK. And do you know who carried out the research?

L Yes, the research was done by Oxford University. I've got the researchers' actual names here somewhere …

T Don't worry about names now, but you'll need to mention them when you write up your assignment. And the other thing you should mention if possible is where the results of this research were published. Do you know that?

L Yes, it was in a scientific journal … called *Nature*, I think. Let me just check … Yes, that's right, *Nature*.

T Fine, carry on.

L OK, well we all know that there are problems with keeping large animals in zoos. When you put lions or tigers, for example, into tiny cages, they often don't breed successfully. That's because of stress, because they're used to having large areas to wander around in. But different animals need different amounts of territory and that's what this research looked at.

J You say different animals need different amounts of territory. Could you give us some specific examples, Lisa?

L Yes, I've got information about four animals; that's the polar bear, lion, grizzly bear and snow leopard. The scientists looked at the average territory these animals had in the wild. And the results were pretty amazing. For example, it turned out that a polar bear has an average territory of around 79,000 square kilometres!

J Did you say 79,000?

L Yes. That's what the report says.

J Wow!

L And the second thing the study looked at was the minimum territory that could support these animals. The minimum territory for a polar bear is still enormous, it's 1,200 square kilometres. On the other hand, grizzly bears only need a minimum territory of 0.5 of a square kilometre, which means they're more likely to do well in a zoo.

J Could you repeat that figure, Lisa?

L Yes. '0.5 of a square kilometre'. OK?

J Thanks.

L The third thing the scientists looked at was the average distance an animal travels in a day. And here it's the lion that comes top. A lion travels 11 kilometers a day, and a polar bear, 8.8. By contrast, grizzly bears only cover about 1.5 kilometres and snow leopards slightly less.

The final thing in the study was the infant mortality rate, that is how many young animals die before they're 30 days old, I think it is. Anyway, the polar bear, has a really high infant mortality rate. It's 65 per cent, which is highest of all. Snow leopards do better, with a rate of 14.3 per cent, but grizzly bears do best of all with 0 per cent infant mortality.

T Is that it?

L Yes, that's as far as I've got.

T Fine, very interesting. But can you draw any conclusions yet?

L Yes, well, basically I think zoos need to decide what kind of animals they should keep. If they're a small city zoo, for example, they should forget about lions, because they need plenty of space, and I'm not sure anyone should keep polar bears at all.

Unit 8, Focus on listening 1

Mobile phone safety (p.84)

T = Tutor; D = David Myers

T So now, just to finish off this morning's session, I've asked the college Health and Safety Officer, David Myers, to say a few words about mobile phone safety. David …

D Thanks, Miranda. Yes, mobiles are an essential part of everyone's life these days, aren't they? And it's hard to believe that hasn't always been the case. Actually, did you know that the first mobile network was only opened in 1979? It's no time at all, really. That was in Japan, by the way. Since then, of course, mobile phone ownership has gone through the roof. In 1990 only about 1 per cent of people in the EU had a mobile, for example, but by 2003 the figure had gone up to about 80 per cent. That's a fantastic increase over such a short space of time.

So why all the fuss about safety? Well, this is quite a hot topic right now, as you probably know. Basically, the concern is that mobile phones work by sending out radio waves and people think that these could damage body tissue and even cause cancer. However, I should say that there's still quite a bit of disagreement among experts about this.

D So, I'd like to pass on to you the latest advice about using mobiles safely. A lot of it's common sense really, I suppose. For example, you should only use the phone when necessary, and you should try to keep your calls short. Don't stay on the phone for hours! Incidentally, you may think the phone is safe when it's on standby, but actually it's still giving off radio-waves. So when you're carrying the phone around, try to keep it away from your body if you can. Put it in your bag or in a backpack, not in your pocket. But then you'll need to be more careful about security, obviously.

Now there are a few things to remember when you're buying a phone. First, look for a model with a long 'talk time'. That means the radio wave emissions it gives out will be less powerful. And less powerful means less risk to health, remember.

You also need to check the 'SAR' value of the phone. That's the amount of radiation that the handset transmits. It's best to avoid phones that have a high 'SAR' value. The higher the 'SAR' value, the more radiation they transmit, which is bad news. Also, don't buy a phone with an internal aerial if you can possibly help it. Many experts think an internal aerial is more dangerous because it's closer to your head. And they think we should keep the aerial as far away from our head as possible.

Something I think I forgot to mention was try not to use your phone when reception is weak. A weak reception means the phone needs more power to communicate to the base station and so the radio wave emissions will be higher.

Finally, there are lots of gadgets around that promise to protect you from harmful radiation – you've probably seen the adverts – but only buy ones that have been independently tested. Otherwise, there's no guarantee at all that they'll work and you'll probably be wasting money.

Well, that's all the advice I have for you now. I hope you'll think about it. Many thanks.

Unit 8, Focus on listening 2

Txt don't talk (p.90)

A = Andy; M =Mary

A Hi, Mary. How are you?

M Fine, thanks. Come in and have a seat. So, how are things going? With the presentation, I mean?

A Not too bad, actually. I found that survey you sent me really useful.

M The one about young people and mobile phones?

A Yes. It's got some interesting facts and figures in it that I think we could use.

M Great.

A They show how incredibly important mobile phones are to young people. For example, did you know that 75 per cent of teenagers use their phones at least once a day.

M Three quarters! That's a lot.

A But actually texting is an even bigger thing with young people nowadays. About 90 per cent of them send at least one text message a day, believe it or not. And if you look at the UK as a whole, people are sending over 2 billion text messages a month. What's so amazing is that it's gone from zero to 2 billion in such a short time

M That's an amazing increase. You know, we could design a graph to show that.

A Great idea! It would be good to have some graphics. By the way, what do you think the peak time for sending text messages is?

M I don't know. Seven thirty? Eight o'clock at night?

A Well, it is at night but apparently it's between ten thirty and eleven.

M That's quite late. I'm surprised!

A What you have to remember about mobiles is that they're part of young people's self-expression. Part of their identity. For example, the way you carry your phone is very important. The most popular place is in your pocket, apparently. And the last place you should keep your phone is on your belt. That's a really big fashion mistake. For most of the teenagers in the survey anyway.

A Now you were going to talk about the different functions of mobile phones, Mary, weren't you? Which functions did you decide to cover?

M Well, the most popular, obviously, is text messaging. But you seem to have a lot of information on that already. So I'll leave that to you, if that's OK.

A Fine, so you won't cover text messaging but … ?

M Well, I'm going to look at using a mobile to take photos. I know not all phones have cameras at the moment, but the number's going up all the time.

A And are you going to deal with sending pictures as well as taking them?

M No. I think it might take too long. But I'm definitely going to look at the kind of games you can play on a mobile because that's the next most popular activity after texting.

A Right. And how about video?

M I think video is still a pretty specialised thing at the moment. Not that many phones have it yet. So I'm not covering that, no. But the other thing I'm going to look at is voicemail. It's not quite as popular with teenagers as the other functions but about two thirds still use it.

M OK, are we nearly done?

A Pretty much so, I think. It's an interesting subject though, isn't it? I mean, you know my younger brother?

M Michael?

A Yes. Well, Michael's 17 now and he's exactly like the teenagers in the survey. He always has the very latest model, and he's always flashing it around. He even uses it as an alarm clock to remind him about appointments and things.

M That's very organised of him! Yeah, my cousin Cindy's like that as well. She told me she has to have the phone with her 24 hours a day. She even keeps it under her pillow when she goes to bed at night! Can you believe it? But the problem is it's easy to run up huge bills. I know someone who got into trouble like that. Linda Hall, do you know her?

A No.

M Well, Linda was sending 20 or 30 texts a day and it was costing over £100 a month.

A What happened?

M Eventually her mother put a limit of £30 on her phone bill. That's all she can spend a month, and she hates it. Anyway, enough of that. I think we've done quite well, don't you? We've sorted out who's doing what. Shall we meet again next week?

Unit 10, Focus on listening 1

Countdown to a healthier life (p.106)

P = Presenter; R = Roger Armstrong

P As you probably know, this is National Stop Smoking Week. And today in the studio we have Roger Armstrong to tell us about some of the benefits of giving up smoking. Roger …

R Thanks, Sally. Yes, I think we've all heard enough bad news. We know about the harmful effects that smoking can have on our bodies and our health. But now for the good news. Let's look at what happens when you finally decide to stop.

Well, the amazing thing is that your body starts to recover almost immediately. For example, both your blood pressure and your pulse will return to normal levels just 20 minutes after your last cigarette. And you'll probably also notice an improvement in your circulation, particularly in your hands and feet. So, if you're the kind of person whose hands and feet go blue at the least sign of cold, this could be the answer!

OK. Then eight hours after you stop, the oxygen level in your blood will return to normal, that is to the normal oxygen level of a non-smoker.

After 24 hours – that's just one day, remember – all the carbon monoxide will have left your body. And this is the point when your lungs begin to clear, to clear out all the debris that's collected in them. So don't be surprised if you develop a cough for a few days. That's a sign that your lungs are recovering.

Now, all the nicotine will leave your body in 48 hours – or two days after you stop. Incredible. And you'll also begin to notice an improvement in your sense of taste and smell. That means you'll be able to enjoy food a lot more. Just one more benefit!

Then after 72 hours, you'll find your breathing has become much easier. And you'll also experience an increase in your energy levels.

As time goes on, your circulation will continue to improve. And then some time between 2 and 12 weeks after you first stopped smoking, you'll notice that walking and exercising have become a lot easier. In fact, exercising can be fun again. You'll soon be cycling or playing tennis without having to keep stopping for a rest.

After 3–9 months, any remaining breathing problems you've had, like coughing or shortness of breath, will get better. In fact, your lungs will increase in efficiency by up to 10 per cent. That means you'll be able to exercise more intensively and also go on for longer.

Looking further ahead, five years after you give up smoking, your risk of having a heart attack will fall to about half that of a smoker.

And finally, ten years after you first gave up, your risk of getting cancer will also fall to about half that of a smoker. Meanwhile, your risk of having a heart attack will now be the same as someone who has never smoked at all.

So, don't delay, give up today! That's the health message I want you all to go away with. It's worth it, believe me! You'll feel some of the benefits almost immediately, but in the long term, you could be saving your life.

Unit 10, Focus on listening 2

Milestones of medicine (p.109)

(*T = Tutor; S = Sara*)

T OK, I think we're all here now. And today Sara, you're doing a presentation on a medical topic, I believe.

S That's right, I wanted to look at some of the key discoveries in medicine over the years. And I thought it would be easy, to be honest, because there's so much information on the Internet, and in the library. But I actually found I had a real problem, because there are just so many amazing developments that it was really difficult to make up my mind which ones to talk about.

I mean where do you start? You can go right back to prehistory if you want. Because people were actually performing operations ten thousand years ago, you know. It's incredible. Anyway, I've picked out some developments that I think are important and I've put them on a time line, which you can see on this chart I've made. The dates are at the bottom, going from left to right. OK?

And we start in 1615 with the clinical thermometer. This was invented in Italy by a physician called Sanctorius. The thermometer made it possible to take human temperature for the first time, which is such an important step in so much medical diagnosis.

Also in the seventeenth century, an Englishman called William Harvey discovered the circulation of the blood. That was in the year 1628. It was a really important breakthrough even though most doctors at the time thought the idea was ridiculous.

Moving on to the next century, 1733 was the year when Stephen Hales, another Englishman, measured blood pressure for the first time. He actually measured the blood pressure of both animals and humans, in fact.

There were lots of medical discoveries during the nineteenth century and one of the most important, in my opinion, was general anaesthetic. Can you imagine having a major operation without anaesthetic? Well, that's how it was for most patients in previous centuries, unfortunately. Then in 1846 general anaesthetic was first used in America.

My last important discovery was in 1895. That's when X-rays were developed in Germany. X-rays have transformed medicine since then but they were actually discovered completely by accident.

S Now I'd like to finish by mentioning a few important medical treatments which have been developed in the last hundred years or so.

The first is **penicillin,** which was discovered in 1928. At first nobody realised how it could be used. Then a few years later, scientists decided to try using penicillin on laboratory mice. That's how they found that penicillin can successfully kill many serious infections.

Next is probably the most common drug of all – something we all reach for when we have a headache – **aspirin.** This was originally extracted from meadowsweet, which is a member of the rose family, and which grows wild in many parts of the country. It had been used for years as a traditional painkiller, in fact.

Beta blockers are an important group of drugs which are used to treat high blood pressure. Drug companies were very excited about them when they were first developed in the 1960s, but a few years later it was found that some patients were suffering heart failure and other damaging conditions. Since then, further research has produced a new generation of beta blockers.

Insulin was discovered by two Canadian scientists who first tried it on a dog which was seriously ill with diabetes. A few hours later the dog sat up and barked. After that success, they treated a young boy whose health improved almost immediately, and nowadays insulin allows diabetics to live almost normal lives.

Cortisone is often used to treat arthritis. The scientists who originally discovered the hormone in the 1940s won a Nobel Prize for their work. Nowadays a synthetic version is used, but doctors have to control the dosage carefully because they've found that patients who take it over a long period run the risk of <u>developing conditions like diabetes or high blood pressure</u>.

T   Thanks, Sara, that was really good. Thank you. I think we'll all take a short break now …

Unit 12, Focus on listening 1

The Opera House Tour (p.130)

T = Tim; E = Erica

E   Hello

T   Erica? Tim here.

E   Oh hi, Tim. Sally said you might ring. You're going to Australia, right? And you wanted some information about tours of the Sydney Opera House?

T   That's right. I haven't got an Internet connection at the moment.

E   No problem. I got a printout from the Opera House website. Let me just get it … right. Opera House Tour. OK. It says: 'This is our most popular tour …', blah blah. 'Visitors are given a fascinating account of the history and <u>architecture</u> of the building.' You see the concert hall, the opera theatre, you hear about the current programme, et cetera. What else do you need to know?

T   Does it say how often the tour goes?

E   Let me see … it's a one-hour tour and, yes, 'it leaves every <u>half hour</u> between 9 a.m. and 5 p.m.'.

T   Right, every half hour. So they're pretty frequent. And does it say how much the tour costs?

E   I think so, yes at the bottom here – adults … <u>23 dollars</u>. But there are some concessionary rates for, um, senior citizens, and also <u>full-time</u> students, plus kids under 16. So remember to take your student card and you'll only have to pay 16 dollars. Which is pretty cheap, actually. But they can also arrange a <u>private tour</u> if you wanted. That's for a group of up to 18 people and it costs, … wait for it! 432 dollars!

E   OK. The other option is the Backstage Tour. Let me read you what it says about that. 'An opportunity to explore behind the scenes at the Opera House. Appear on the stage and see where the orchestra plays.' You also get the chance to chat to some of the <u>technical</u> staff and maybe even some performers, if you're lucky …

T   Sounds really great but how long does that one take?

E   Um, that's <u>two hours</u>, so twice as long as the first one. But there's an early start – it goes at 7 a.m.

T   And how much is that?

E   Let me see … <u>a hundred and forty dollars</u>.

T   That's per person, right?

E   Yes, per person. I think it's something pretty special. And apparently, included in the ticket price, you also get a light <u>breakfast</u>. Which would be very welcome, I should think, after that early start!

T   Right. I'll have to give it some thought.

E   Well, anyway, if you are interested, I'd try and book well in advance if you can. I think the tours get quite booked up.

T   OK.

E   There's a number you can call for bookings or if you want more information. Have you got a pen handy?

T   Yup. Fire away.

E   OK. It's <u>9250 7250</u>. That's Sydney, obviously. Did you get that? 9250 7250.

T   Got it. That's brilliant, Erica. Thanks a lot.

Unit 12, Focus on listening 2

The Itaipu Dam (p.131)

Hello and welcome to this, the fourth in our series of public lectures on Big Buildings. Today we're going to take a look at the Itaipu Dam in South America. You may not know too much about Itaipu but it's been named one of the 'Seven Wonders of the Modern World' by the American Society of Civil Engineers. And in this lecture, I hope to explain some of the reasons why.

OK, let's begin with a few facts. First of all, where exactly is the Itaipu Dam? Well, it's on the Parana River, close to the border between Brazil and Paraguay. Construction began in 1975 and the dam was only finished in <u>1982</u>. Two years later it started generating electricity and it's now one of the largest hydro-electric power plants in the world. The total cost of building was <u>20 billion</u> dollars. That's right, 20 billion!

In design, it's what is called a gravity dam, which means it relies on its immense weight for stability. The main section is made of <u>concrete</u>, actually 15 times the amount of concrete that was used in creating the Channel Tunnel between England and France.

To give you an idea of size, the dam is 7.8 kilometres long, with a <u>height</u> of 196 metres. The reservoir behind the dam is huge – almost fifteen hundred square kilometres and the reservoir <u>capacity</u> is 1.02 trillion cubic feet. With such a massive capacity, no wonder it took fourteen days to fill!

This dam really is an amazing feat of engineering. Engineers actually had to change the course of the Parana, which is the seventh largest river in the world, and move 50 million tons of earth and rock in the process.

With any success story, I suppose there are bound to be a few problems. One is that the Itaipu Dam sometimes gets blocked with mud and silt, which is expensive to clear. But more seriously, <u>this mud and silt carries bacteria, which can be transmitted in the water and cause illness in the people who use it</u>. So it's essential the water's kept clean. The other main problem was that when the land was originally flooded to create the reservoir, they destroyed <u>a large area of rainforest, which was home to many birds and other forest creatures and sadly they died</u>. Since then, however, seven new protected areas have been created for wildlife.

OK, now before I go on, has anyone got any questions? … No? Well, I'd like to look at the construction of the dam in a bit more detail. So, if you could all look at the cross-section of a dam on the sheet I gave out … OK? Look at the left side, which is the side facing the reservoir. Can you see the point at the very bottom of the dam on the upstream face? That's called the '<u>heel</u>', H double E, L, just like part of your foot. And the same point at the bottom of the downstream face of the dam is called, anyone care to guess? That's it, the '<u>toe</u>' also like the toe on your foot. What else should I mention? Yes, the top of a dam, that's the part you can see above water, the 'crest', and then the base or ground on which the dam is built is the '<u>foundation</u>'. I think that's all you need for now.

Now, I've got a few more diagrams … if you'll just bear with me while I find out how to work this projector …